ORPHEUS DESCENDING

A PLAY IN THREE ACTS BY
TENNESSEE WILLIAMS

★

DRAMATISTS
PLAY SERVICE
INC.

SPECIAL NOTE

Anyone receiving permission to produce ORPHEUS DESCENDING is required to give credit to the Author as sole and exclusive Author of the Play on the title page of all programs distributed in connection with performances of the Play and in all instances in which the title of the Play appears, including printed or digital materials for advertising, publicizing or otherwise exploiting the Play and/or a production thereof. The following acknowledgment must appear on the title page in all programs distributed in connection with performances of the Play:

ORPHEUS DESCENDING is presented by arrangement with Dramatists Play Service, Inc. on behalf of The University of the South, Sewanee, Tennessee.

ALL TENNESSEE WILLIAMS PLAYS

The Play must be performed as published in the DPS authorized edition. It is understood that there will be no nudity in the Play unless specifically indicated in the script and that nothing in the stage presentation or stage business will alter the spirit of the Play as written.

SPECIAL NOTE ON SONGS AND RECORDINGS

Dramatists Play Service, Inc. neither holds the rights to nor grants permission to use any songs or recordings mentioned in the Play. Permission for performances of copyrighted songs, arrangements or recordings mentioned in this Play is not included in our license agreement. The permission of the copyright owner(s) must be obtained for any such use. For any songs and/or recordings mentioned in the Play, other songs, arrangements, or recordings may be substituted provided permission from the copyright owner(s) of such songs, arrangements or recordings is obtained; or songs, arrangements or recordings in the public domain may be substituted.

ORPHEUS DESCENDING was first presented by The Producers Theatre at the Martin Beck Theatre, New York City, on March 21, 1957. It was directed by Harold Clurman; the set was designed by Boris Aronson, and the lighting by Feder. The cast was as follows:

DOLLY HAMMA	Elizabeth Eustis
BEULAH BINNINGS	Jane Rose
PEE WEE BINNINGS	Warren Kemmerling
DOG HAMMA	David Clarke
CAROL CUTRERE	Lois Smith
EVA TEMPLE	Nell Harrison
SISTER TEMPLE	Mary Farrell
UNCLE PLEASANT	John Marriott
VAL XAVIER	Cliff Robertson
VEE TALBOTT	Joanna Roos
LADY TORRANCE	Maureen Stapleton
JABE TORRANCE	Crahan Denton
SHERIFF TALBOTT	R. G. Armstrong
MR. DUBINSKY	Beau Tilden
WOMAN	Janice Mars
DAVID CUTRERE	Robert Webber
NURSE PORTER	Virgilia Chew
FIRST MAN	Albert Henderson
SECOND MAN	Charles Tyner

Production Stage Manager, JAMES GELB
Stage Manager, BEAU TILDEN

The entire action of the play takes place in a general drygoods store and part of a connecting "confectionery" in a small Southern town, during a rainy season, late winter, and early spring.

Act I

Scene 1: Late dusk.
Scene 2: A couple of hours later that night.

INTERMISSION

Act II

Scene 1: Afternoon, a few weeks later.
Scene 2: Late that night.

INTERMISSION

Act III

Scene 1: Early morning, the Saturday before Easter.
Scene 2: Sunset, the same day.
Scene 3: Half an hour later.

NOTE ON MUSIC

The song "Heavenly Grass" is published by G. Schirmer, Inc., 180 Madison Avenue, New York, NY 10016. Permission for the use of the song in connection with amateur production of ORPHEUS DESCENDING must be obtained from Schirmer.

*I, too, am beginning to feel an immense need
to become a savage and create a new world.*

—August Strindberg,
in letter to Paul Gauguin

ORPHEUS DESCENDING

ACT I

SCENE 1

The set represents in non-realistic fashion a general dry-goods store and part of a connecting "confectionery" in a small Southern town. The ceiling is high and the upper walls are dark, as if streaked with moisture, and cobwebbed. Two great dusty windows upstage offer a view of disturbing emptiness then fades into late dusk. The action of the play occurs during a rainy season, late winter and early spring, and sometimes the window turns opaque but glistening silver with sheets of rain. "TORRANCE MERCANTILE STORE" is lettered on the window in gilt of old-fashioned design. The entrance door (double doors) is U. C. between the windows. Merchandise is represented very sparsely and it is not realistic. Bolts of Pepperell and percale stand upright on large spools, the black skeleton of a dressmaker's dummy stands in upper R. window. A counter runs from U. L. C. to foot of stairs D. L. C. There are stairs D. L. that lead to a landing and disappear above it, and on the landing there is a sinister-looking artificial palm tree in a greenish-brown jardiniere, and a bench. But the confectionery R., which is seen partly through a wide arched door D. R. is shadowy and poetic as some inner dimension of the play. Small tables and chairs in the confectionery. Another, much smaller, playing area is a tiny bedroom alcove D. L. under stair landing, which is usually masked by an oriental drapery which is worn dim but bears the formal design of gold tree with scarlet fruit and fantastic birds. A cot bed R. in the alcove. There is a platform covering the alcove extreme D. L., which must be strong enough to be used for all entrances and exits to and from Jabe's room off U. L. A stool stands between the D.S. end of the counter and the stairs. There is a wall telephone behind the D.S. end of the counter, just U.S. of the stairs. The cash register is near the telephone on a shelf against the wall behind the counter. Shelves for the merchandise are against the L. wall and against the rear wall, L. of the window. A clothes rack is D. L., just L. of the entrance to the alcove. In the alcove, against the R. wall is a cot bed. There is also a mirror in the alcove. A chair U. L., above the counter. A light over the counter. D. R. a jukebox, to R. of archway to confectionery. In front of the confectionery archway are chairs for shoe fitting, with a stool in front of them. The shoe-fitting chairs are two wooden theater seats with center arm rest removed. Stacks of shoeboxes just above shoe-fitting chair, and another stack of boxes under the stairs D. L. The store area to just above the shoe chairs is on a raised platform, with a post at the D. R. corner of this, the L. side of the archway to confectionery is formed by this post. On the U.S. side of this post is a button which is used when actors switch on or off lights in confectionery. (Not practical.)

Guitar music is heard offstage.

Two youngish middle-aged women, Dolly and Beulah, are laying out a buffet supper on a pink-and-gray veined marble-topped table with gracefully curved black iron legs, brought into the main area to D. R. C. from the confectionery. A chair L. of table. A vase of flowers is on table. They are the wives of small planters and tastelessly overdressed in a somewhat bizarre fashion. Music fades out. A train whistles in the distance. [Sound Cue 1.] The women pause in their occupations at the tables and rush to the archway D. R., crying out harshly:

BEULAH. Pee Wee!

DOLLY. Dawg! Cannonball is comin' into th' depot!

BEULAH. You all git down to th' depot an' meet that train!

Their husbands, Dog and Pee Wee, enter from confectionery D. R. and slouch through—heavy, red-faced men in clothes that are too tight for them or too loose, and mud-stained boots.

PEE WEE. I fed that one-armed bandit a hunnerd nickels an' it coughed up five.

DOG. Must have had indigestion.

PEE WEE. I'm gonna speak to Jabe about them slots.

They go out the front door U. C. Beulah sits in chair L. of table.

DOLLY. I guess Jabe Torrance has got more to worry about than the slot machines and pinball games in that confectionery.

BEULAH. You're not tellin' a lie. Last time I seen Dr. Johnny I ast him what was the facks about Jabe Torrance's operation in Memphis. Well—

DOLLY. What'd he tell you, Beulah?

BEULAH. He said the worse thing a doctor ever can say.

DOLLY. What's that, Beulah?

BEULAH. Nothin' a-tall, not a spoken word did he utter! He just looked at me with those big dark eyes of his and shook his haid like this!

DOLLY. *(Sitting in shoe-fitting chair D. R.; with doleful satisfaction.)* I guess he signed Jabe Torrance's death-warrant with just that single silent motion of his haid.

BEULAH. That's exactly what passed through my mind. I understand that they cut him open—

She pauses to taste something on the table.

DOLLY. —An' sewed him right back up!—that's what I heard—

BEULAH. I didn't know these olives had seeds in them!

DOLLY. You thought they was stuffed?

BEULAH. Uh-huh. Where's the Temple sisters?

DOLLY. Where d'you think?

BEULAH. *(Rises, crosses to foot of stairs D. L.)* Snoopin' aroun' upstairs. If Lady catches 'em at it she'll give those two old maids a touch of her tongue! She's not a dago for nothin'!

9

DOLLY. Ha, ha, no! You spoke a true word, honey. …Well, I was surprised when I wint up myself!

BEULAH. You wint up you'self?

DOLLY. I did and so did you because I seen you, Beulah.

BEULAH. I never said that I didn't. Curiosity is a human instinct. *(Crossing back to above table C.)*

DOLLY. Y'know what it seemed like to me up there? A county jail! I swear to goodness it didn't seem to me like a place for white people to live in!—that's the truth…

BEULAH. *(Darkly.)* Well, I wasn't surprised. Jabe Torrance bought that woman.

DOLLY. Bought her?

BEULAH. *(Crossing to between table and post R.)* Yais, he bought her, when she was a girl of eighteen! He bought her and bought her cheap because she'd been thrown over and her heart was broken by David Cutrere. …You know Carol Cutrere's big brother. …*Oh*, what a—*Mmmm*, what a—beautiful thing he was. …And those two met like you struck two stones together and made a fire! Well, he quit Lady the summer the Mystic Crew set fire to her father's wine garden for sellin' liquor to niggers! And Lady's father was burned alive fightin' the fire.

DOLLY. Lawd have mercy!

BEULAH. *(Crossing to Dolly.)* Uh-huh, I second the motion. But after that happened, David Cutrere didn't want no further connection with Lady, and thrown her over…

> *They are startled by sudden light laughter from the dim upstage area. The light changes on the stage to mark a division.*
>
> *The women turn to see Carol Cutrere in the doorway U. C. She is past thirty and, lacking prettiness, she has an odd, fugitive beauty which is stressed, almost to the point of fantasy, by a style of makeup with which a dancer named Valli has lately made such an impression in the Bohemian centers of France and Italy, the face and lips powdered white and the eyes outlined and exaggerated with black pencil and the lids tinted blue. She wears a trenchcoat over a black dress, and is*

barefoot. She carries her shoes. Her family name is the oldest and most distinguished in the county.

DOLLY. Speakin' of the Cutreres!

BEULAH. *(Moves away to D. R.)* Somebody don't seem to know that the store is closed.

DOLLY. *(Rises.)* Can you understand how anybody would deliberately make themselves look fantastic as that?

BEULAH. Some people have to show off, anything on earth to attract attention.

> *During these lines, just loud enough for her to hear them, Carol has crossed to the payphone behind counter and deposited a coin.*

CAROL. I want Tulane 0370 in New Orleans. What? Oh. Hold on a minute.

> *Eva Temple is descending the stairs, slowly, as if awed by Carol's appearance. Carol rings open the cashbox and removes some coins, returns to deposit coins in phone.*

BEULAH. She helped herself to money out of the cashbox.

CAROL. Hello, Sister.

EVA. *(Nearing foot of stairs.)* I'm Eva.

CAROL. Hello, Eva.

EVA. —Hello… *(Then in a loud whisper as she crosses to Beulah and Dolly; passing Carol like a timid child skirting a lion cage.)* She took money out of the cashbox.

DOLLY. Oh, she can do as she pleases, she's a Cutrere!

BEULAH. —Shoot…

EVA. What is she doin' barefooted?

BEULAH. The last time she was arrested on the highway, they say that she was naked under her coat.

CAROL. *(To operator.)* I'm waiting. *(Then to women.)* —I caught the heel of my slipper in that rotten boardwalk out there and it broke right off. *(Raises slippers in hand.)* They say if you break the heel of your slipper in the morning it means you'll meet the love of your life before dark. But it was already dark when I broke the heel

11

of my slipper. Maybe that means I'll meet the love of my life before daybreak.

>*The quality of her voice is curiously clear and childlike. Sister Temple appears on stair landing.*

SISTER. Wasn't that them?

EVA. *(Moving U. R. C.)* No, it was Carol Cutrere!

CAROL. *(At phone.)* Just keep on ringing, please, he's probably drunk.

>*Sister crosses by her as Eva did and goes to Eva.*

Sometimes it takes quite a while to get through the living room furniture…

SISTER. —She a *sight*?

EVA. Uh-*huh*! A sight to be seen!

CAROL. Bertie?—Carol!—Hi, doll! Did you trip over something? I heard a crash. Well, I'm leaving right now, I'm already on the highway and everything's fixed, I've got my allowance back on condition that I remain forever away from Two River County! I had to blackmail them a little. I came to dinner with my eyes made up and my crazy black sequin jacket and Betsy Boo, my brother's wife, said, "Carol, you going out to a fancy dress ball?" I said, "Oh, no, I'm just going jooking tonight up and down the Dixie Highway between here and Memphis like I used to when I lived here." Why, honey, she flew so fast you couldn't see her passing and came back in with the ink still wet on the check! And this will be done once a month as long as I stay away from Two River County…

>*She laughs gaily—looks at the women—Dolly sits in shoe chair.*

Oh, honey, I'm driving straight through, not even stopping for pick-ups unless you need one! I'll meet you in the Starlite Lounge before it closes, or if I'm irresistibly delayed, I'll certainly join you for coffee at the Morning Call before the all-night places have closed for the day. …Bye-bye.

>*She laughs uncertainly and hangs up.*

—let's see, now…

>*Carol removes a revolver from her trenchcoat pocket and crosses to look for cartridges back of counter.*

EVA. What she looking for?

SISTER. Ask her.

EVA. *(Advancing.)* What're you looking for, Carol?

CAROL. Cartridges for my revolver.

> *Eva moves back to Sister.*

DOLLY. She don't have a license to carry a pistol.

BEULAH. She don't have a license to drive a car.

CAROL. When I stop for someone I want to be sure it's someone I want to stop for.

DOLLY. Sheriff Talbott ought to know about this when he gits back from the depot.

CAROL. Tell him, ladies. I've already given him notice that if he ever attempts to stop me again on the highway, I'll shoot it out with him…

> *She points revolver—the sisters retreat toward confectionery.*

BEULAH. When anybody has trouble with the law—

> *Her sentence is interrupted by a panicky scream from Eva, immediately repeated by Sister. The Temple sisters scramble upstairs to the landing. Dolly also rises, cries out and turns, covering her face. A Negro "Conjure Man" (Uncle Pleasant) has entered D. R. through the confectionery into the store. His tattered garments are fantastically bedizened with many talismans and good-luck charms of shell and bone and feather. His blue-black skin is daubed with cryptic signs in white paint.*

DOLLY. Git him out, git him out, he's going to mark my baby!

BEULAH. Oh, shoot, Dolly…

> *Dolly has now fled after the Temple sisters, to the third step of the stairs. The Conjure Man advances with a soft, rapid, toothless mumble of words that sound like wind in dry grass. He is holding out something in his shaking hand.*

It's just that old crazy "conjure man" from Blue Mountain. He cain't mark your baby.

> *Beulah moves away to below jukebox D. R.*

CAROL. *(Coming from behind counter to U. C.; very high and clear voice.)* Come here, Uncle, and let me see what you've got there. Oh,

13

it's a bone of some kind. No, I don't want to touch it, it isn't clean yet, there's still some flesh clinging to it.

Women make sounds of revulsion.

You leave it a long time on a bare rock in the rain and the sun till every sign of corruption is burned and washed away from it, and then it will be a good charm, Uncle.

The Conjure Man makes a ducking obeisance and shuffles slowly back to the confectionery.

Hey, Uncle Pleasant, give us the Choctaw Cry.

Conjure Man stops in confectionery.

He's part Choctaw, he knows the Choctaw cry.

SISTER. Don't let him holler in *here*!

CAROL. Come on, Uncle Pleasant, *you* know it!

She takes coat off—sits on R. windowsill. She starts to cry herself. He throws back his head and completes it: a series of barking sounds that rise to a high, sustained note of wild intensity. (The Choctaw Cry "bit" will be used again in the play but it has to be used, then, in a totally different fashion, probably in a much more serious one. It must not sound like Tarzan.)

Eva and Sister exit upstairs L. But Dolly stays on third step up.

Just then, as though the cry had brought him, Val enters the store U. C. He is a young man, about 30, who has a kind of wild beauty about him that the cry would suggest. He does not wear Levi's or a T-shirt, he has on a pair of dark serge pants, glazed from long wear and not excessively tight-fitting. His remarkable garment is a snakeskin jacket, mottled white, black, and gray. He carries a guitar, which is covered with inscriptions. Carol, looking at the young man:

…Thanks, Uncle…

Val observes with a calm interest. Carol smiles. Uncle Pleasant waits for his dollar.

BEULAH. *Hey, old man, you! Choctaw! Conjure man! Will you go out-a this sto'? So they can come back down stairs?*

Carol hands Uncle Pleasant a dollar—he goes out R. cackling. Vee Talbott enters the store U. C. with the hem of her skirt dragging loose. Val moves above counter U. L. Vee is a heavy, vague woman in her forties. She does primitive oil paintings and carries one of these framed canvases into the store with her, saying vaguely...

VEE. I got m' skirt caught in th' door of the Chevrolet an' I'm afraid I tore it.

Beulah and Dolly greet Vee in various laconic drawls, their interest being focused on the man with her.

Is it dark in here or am I losin' my eyesight? I been painting all day, finished a picture in a ten-hour stretch, just stopped a few minutes fo' coffee and went back to it again while I had a clear vision. I think I got it this time. But I'm so exhausted I could drop in my tracks. There's nothing more exhausting than that kind of work on earth, it's not so much that it tires your body out, but it leaves you drained inside. Y'know what I mean? Inside? Like you was burned out by something? Well! Still!—You feel you've accomplished something when you're through with it, sometimes you feel—*elevated*! How are you, Dolly?

Vee crosses to front of counter just above Dolly.

DOLLY. All right, Mrs. Talbott.

VEE. That's good. How are *you*, Beulah?

BEULAH. Oh, I'm all right, I reckon.

VEE. Still can't make out much. Who is that there? *(Indicates Carol's figure by the window.)*

A significant silence greets this enquiry of Vee's.

(Suddenly.) OH! I thought her folks had got her out of the county...

Carol utters a very light, slightly rueful laugh, her eyes drifting back to the man as she moves back into confectionery.

Jabe and Lady back yet?

DOLLY. Pee Wee an' Dawg have gone to the depot to meet 'em.

VEE. Aw. Well, I'm just in time. I brought my new picture with me, the paint isn't dry on it yet. I thought that Lady might want to hang it up in Jabe's room while he's convalescin' from the operation 'cause

15

after a close shave with death, people like to be reminded of spiritual things. Huh? Yes! This is the Holy Ghost ascending…

DOLLY. *(Looking at canvas.)* You didn't put a head on it.

VEE. The head was a blaze of light, that's all I saw in my vision.

DOLLY. Who's the young man with yuh?

VEE. Aw, excuse me, I'm too worn out to have manners. This is Mr. Valentine Xavier. Mrs. Hamma and Mrs.—I'm sorry, Beulah, I never *can* get y' last *name*!

> *Val moves down to above table c. on introductions. He has put guitar down above counter.*

BEULAH. *(Crossing to u. and r. of Val.)* I fo'give you. My name is Beulah Binnings.

VAL. What shall I do with this here?

> *He has been holding a china bowl with a glazed paper cover on it.*

VEE. Aw, that bowl of sherbet. I thought that Jabe might need something light an' digestible, so I brought him this sherbet. Pineapple.

DOLLY. Better put it in the icebox before it starts to melt.

BEULAH. *(Looking under napkin that covers bowl.)* I'm afraid you're lockin' th' stable after the horse is gone.

DOLLY. Aw, is it melted already?

BEULAH. Reduced to juice.

VEE. Aw, shoot. Well, put it on ice anyhow, it might thicken up.

> *Women are still watching Val.*

Where's the icebox?

BEULAH. In the confectionery.

VEE. I thought that Lady had closed the confectionery.

BEULAH. Yes, but the Frigidaire's still there.

> *Val goes out r. through confectionery.*

VEE. Mr. Xavier is a stranger in our midst. His car broke down in that storm last night and I let him sleep in the jail. He's lookin' for work and I thought I'd introduce him to Lady an' Jabe because if Jabe can't work they're going to need somebody to help out in th' store.

16

BEULAH. That's a good idea.

DOLLY. Uh-huh.

BEULAH. Well, come on in, you all, it don't look like they're comin' straight home from the depot anyhow.

DOLLY. Maybe that wasn't the Cannonball Express.

BEULAH. Or maybe they stopped off fo' Pee Wee to buy some liquor.

DOLLY. Yeah...

> *They move past Carol and out of sight, exiting through the confectionery R. Val reenters R., crosses to counter—puts guitar down. Carol has risen. Now she crosses into the main store area, watching Val with the candid curiosity of one child observing another. He pays no attention but concentrates on his belt buckle, which he is repairing with a pocket knife.*

CAROL. What're you fixing?

VAL. Belt buckle.

CAROL. Boys like you are always fixing something. Could you fix my slipper?

VAL. What's wrong with your slipper?

CAROL. Why are you pretending not to remember me?

VAL. It's hard to remember someone you never met.

CAROL. Then why'd you look so startled when you saw me?

VAL. Did I?

CAROL. I thought for a moment you'd run back out the door.

VAL. The sight of a woman can make me walk in a hurry but I don't think it's ever made me run.—You're standing in my light.

CAROL. *(Moving aside slightly.)* Oh, excuse me. Better?

VAL. Thanks...

CAROL. *(Going behind counter.)* Can I see your wristwatch?

VAL. —Huh?

> *He has covered his wristwatch with his sleeve.*

CAROL. Never mind. I saw it. It's my cousin Bertie's Rolex chronometer that tells not just the time of day but the day of the week and the month and even the phases of the moon.

Val stares as if mystified.

Keep it. I won't say a word about it, but I can prove that I know you, if I have to. It was New Year's Eve in New Orleans and you—

VAL. *(Sitting in chair L. of table.)* I need a small pair of pliers.

CAROL. —Y' had on that jacket and a snake ring with a ruby eye which I see on your hand now.

Val continues to work on belt buckle.

(Smiling gently.) You told us that it was a gift from a lady osteopath that you'd met somewhere in your travels and that any time you were broke you'd wire this lady osteopath collect, and no matter how far you were or how long it was since you'd seen her, she'd send you a money order for twenty-five dollars with the same sweet message each time. "I love you. When will you come back?" And to prove the story, not that it was difficult to believe it, you took the latest of these sweet messages from your wallet for us to see…

She throws back her head with soft laughter. He looks away still further and busies himself with the belt buckle. Music fades in from guitar offstage.

—We followed you through five places before we made contact with you and I was the one that made contact. I went up to the bar where you were standing and touched your jacket and said, "What stuff is this made of," and when you said it was snakeskin, I said, "I wish you'd told me before I touched it." And you said something not nice. You said maybe that will learn you to hold back your hands. I was drunk by that time which was after midnight. *(Coming from behind counter to Val.)* Do you remember what I said to you? I said, "What on earth can you do on this earth but catch at whatever comes near you, with both your hands, until your fingers are broken?" I'd never said that before, or even consciously thought it, but afterwards it seemed like the truest thing that my lips had ever spoken, what on earth can you do but catch at whatever comes near you and hold on to it until your fingers are broken. …You gave me a quick, sober look. I think you nodded slightly, and then you picked up your guitar and began to sing. After singing you passed the kitty. Whenever paper money was dropped in the kitty you blew a whistle.

Val rises—crosses D. R.

My cousin Bertie and I dropped in five dollars, you blew the whistle five times and then sat down at our table for a drink, Schenley's with Seven Up. You showed us all those signatures on your guitar… Any correction so far?

Music fades out.

VAL. *(Sitting in shoe chair.)* Why are you so anxious to prove I know you?

CAROL. *(Crossing and sitting on shoe stool beside him.)* Because I want to know you better and better! I'd like to go out jooking with you tonight.

VAL. What's jooking?

CAROL. You know what that is? That's where you get in a car and drink a little and drive a little and stop and dance a little to a juke-box and then you drink a little more and drive a little more and stop and dance a little more to a jukebox and then you stop dancing and you just drink and drive and then you stop driving and just drink, and then, finally, you stop drinking…

VAL. —What do you do, then?

CAROL. That depends on the weather and who you're jooking with. If it's a clear night you spread a blanket among the memorial stones on Cypress Hill, which is the local bone orchard, but if it's not a fair night, and this one certainly isn't, why, usually then you go to the Wildwood cabins between here and Sunset on the highway…

VAL. *(Rises—crossing to counter.)* —That's about what I figured. But I don't go that route. Heavy drinking and smoking the weed and shacking with strangers is okay for kids in their twenties but this is my thirtieth birthday and I'm all through with that route. *(Looks up with dark eyes.)* I'm not young anymore.

CAROL. *(Rises—crossing up to R. window.)* You're young at thirty— I hope so! I'm twenty-seven!

VAL. Naw, you're not young at thirty if you've been on a goddam party since you were fifteen!

Val picks up his guitar and sings and plays "Heavenly Grass"—stops in middle of song.

CAROL. Go on.

VAL. My throat's a little dry.

> *Carol has taken a pint of bourbon from her trenchcoat pocket and she passes it to him.*

CAROL. Here.

> *She is very close to him. Vee enters D. R. through confectionery and says sharply:*

VEE. Mr. Xavier don't drink.

CAROL. Oh, ex-cuse *me*!

> *She crosses away to D. R. and leans on jukebox.*

VEE. And if you behaved yourself better your father would not be paralyzed in bed!

> *She and Val move above counter. Sound of car off L. [Sound Cue 2.] Women come running with various cries. Beulah rushes on from confectionery R., followed by Dolly. Both ad libbing excitedly. Lady enters U. C., nodding to the women and holding the door open for her husband and the men (Sheriff Talbott, Pee Wee, and Dog) following him. She greets the women in almost toneless murmurs, as if too tired to speak. She could be any age between 35 and 45 in appearance, but her figure is youthful. Her face taut. She is a woman who met with emotional disaster in her girlhood: verges on hysteria under a strain. Her voice is often shrill and her body tense. But when in repose, a girlish softness emerges again and she looks ten years younger.*

BEULAH. Well, Lady!

LADY. Come in, Jabe! We've got a reception committee here to meet us. They've set up a buffet supper.

> *She sits in chair L. of table. Jabe enters U. C. A gaunt, wolfish man, gray and yellow. The women chatter idiotically. Sheriff Talbott goes up and waits on the landing. Pee Wee and Dog stand U. C., closing doors behind them.*

BEULAH. Well, look who's here!

DOLLY. Well, *Jabe!*

BEULAH. I don't think he's been sick. I think he's been to Miami. Look at that wonderful color in his face!

DOLLY. I never seen him look better in my life!

BEULAH. Who does he think he's foolin'? Ha ha ha!—not *me!*

JABE. *(Crossing to lower end of counter.)* Whew, Jesus—I'm mighty—tired…

> *An uncomfortable silence, everyone staring greedily at the dying man with his tense wolfish smile and nervous cough.*

PEE WEE. Well, Jabe, we been feedin' lots of nickels to those one-arm bandits in there.

DOG. An' that pinball machine is hotter'n a pistol.

PEE WEE. Ha ha.

> *Eva Temple appears on stairs and screams for her sister.*

EVA. Sistuh! Sistuh! Sistuh! Cousin Jabe's here!

> *A loud clatter upstairs and shrieks.*

JABE. Jesus…

> *Eva, rushing downstairs, stops short and bursts into tears. Very rapid, all overlapping:*

LADY. Oh, cut that out, Eva Temple!—What were you doin' upstairs?

EVA. *(Coming down last step and crossing to Jabe.)* I can't help it, it's so good to see him, it's so wonderful to see our cousin again, oh, Jabe, *blessed!*

SISTER. *(Coming downstairs.)* Where's Jabe, where's precious Jabe? Where's our precious cousin?

EVA. Right here, Sister!

SISTER. Well, bless your old sweet life, and lookit the color he's got in his face, will you?

BEULAH. I just told him he looks like he's been to Miami and got a Florida suntan, haha ha!

> *The above six speeches by women are very rapid, all overlapping.*

JABE. I ain't been out in no sun an' if you all will excuse me I'm gonna do my celebratin' upstairs in bed because I'm kind of—worn out.

He goes creakily to foot of steps while Eva and Sister sob into
their handkerchiefs behind him. He stops, turns to Lady.

—I see they's been some changes made here. Uh-huh. Uh-huh. How come the shoe department's back here now?

Lady rises. Instant hostility as if habitual between them.

LADY. We always had a problem with light in this store.

JABE. So you put the shoe department further away from the window? That's sensible. A very intelligent solution to the problem, Lady.

LADY. *(A step toward him.)* Jabe, you know I told you we got a fluorescent tube coming to put back here.

JABE. Uh-huh. Uh-huh. Well. Tomorrow I'll get me some niggers to help me move the shoe department back front.

LADY. You do whatever you want to, it's your store.

JABE. Uh-huh. Uh-huh. I'm glad you reminded me of it.

Lady turns sharply away. Jabe starts upstairs. Pee Wee and
Dog follow him up and off L., joined by Sheriff Talbott. The
women huddle and whisper in the store. Lady sinks wearily
into chair at table.

BEULAH. That man will never come down those stairs again!

DOLLY. Never in this world, honey.

BEULAH. He has th' death sweat on him!

Sister sobs.

EVA. Sister, Sister!

BEULAH. *(Crossing to Lady.)* Lady, I don't suppose you feel much like talking about it right now but Pee Wee and me are so worried.

DOLLY. Dawg and me are worried sick about it.

LADY. —About what?

BEULAH. Jabe's operation in Memphis. Was it successful?

DOLLY. Wasn't it successful?

Lady stares at them blindly. The women, except Carol, close
avidly about her, tense with morbid interest.

SISTER. Was it too late for surgical interference?

EVA. Wasn't it successful? We hope and pray it ain't hopeless.

All their faces wear faint, unconscious smiles. Lady looks from face to face, then utters a slight, startled laugh and a loud measured knock begins on the floor above and Lady springs up from the table and crosses to the stairs.

LADY. *(As if in flight.)* Excuse me, I have to go up, Jabe's knocking for me.

Lady goes upstairs. The women gaze after her. Then Vee signals Val to wait and goes upstairs. The Temple sisters start to follow her up but stop on stair landing as Carol starts to speak. Beulah and Dolly have started out R. but stop in confectionery and listen. Carol, crossing to R. window, puts on coat. Val lights a cigarette and crosses down below counter.

CAROL. *(Suddenly and clearly, in the silence.)* Speaking of knocks, I have a knock in my engine. It goes knock, knock, and I say who's there. I don't know whether I'm in communication with some dead ancestor or the motor's about to drop out and leave me stranded in the dead of night on the Dixie Highway. *(Crossing to Val.)* Do you have any knowledge of mechanics? I'm sure you do. Would you be sweet and take a short drive with me? So you could hear that knock?

VAL. I don't have time.

CAROL. What have you got to do?

VAL. I'm waiting to see about a job in this store.

He sits on a stool below counter.

CAROL. I'm offering you a job.

VAL. I want a job that pays.

CAROL. I expect to pay you.

Women whisper loudly in the background.

VAL. Maybe sometime tomorrow.

CAROL. I can't stay here overnight, I'm not allowed to stay overnight in this county.

Whispers rise. The word "corrupt" is distinguished.

(Without turning, smiling very brightly.) What are they saying about me? Can you hear what those women are saying about me?

The Temple sisters sit down on a bench on landing.

VAL.   —Play it cool...

CAROL.   I don't like playing it cool! What are they saying about me? That I'm corrupt?

VAL.   If you don't want to be talked about, why do you make up like that, why do you—

CAROL.   *To show off!*

VAL.   What?

CAROL.   *I'm an exhibitionist!* I want to be noticed, seen, heard, felt! I want them to know I'm alive! Don't you want them to know you're alive?

VAL.   I want to live and I don't care if they know I'm alive or not.

CAROL.   Then why do you play a guitar?

VAL.   Why do you make a goddam show of yourself?

CAROL.   That's right, for the same reason.

VAL.   We don't go the same route...

He turns away from her.

CAROL.   I used to be what they call a Christ-bitten reformer. You know what that is?—A kind of benign exhibitionist. ...I delivered stump speeches, wrote letters of protest, about the gradual massacre of the colored majority in the county. I thought it was wrong for pellagra and slow starvation to cut them down when the cotton crop failed from army worm or boll weevil or too much rain in summer. I wanted to, tried to, put up free clinics, I squandered the money my mother left me on it. And when that Willie McGee thing came along—he was sent to the chair for having improper relations with a white whore— *(Her voice is like a passionate incantation.)* I made a fuss about it. I put on a potato sack and set out for the capital on foot. This was in winter. I walked barefoot in this burlap sack to deliver a personal protest to the governor of the state. Oh, I suppose it was partly exhibitionism on my part, but it wasn't completely exhibitionism, there was something else in it, too. You know how far I got? Six miles out of town—hooted, jeered at, even spit on!—every step of the way—and then arrested! Guess what for? Lewd vagrancy! Uh-huh, that was the charge, "lewd vagrancy," because they said that potato sack I had on was not a respectable garment. …Well, all that was a pretty long time ago, and now I'm not a reformer anymore. I'm just a "lewd vagrant." And I'm showing the S.O.B.s how lewd a "lewd vagrant" can be if she puts her whole heart in it like I do mine! All right. I've told you my story, the story of an exhibitionist.

She throws her scarf around his neck and crouches beside him.

Now I want you to do something for me. Take me out to Cypress Hill in my car. And we'll hear the dead people talk. They do talk there. They chatter together like birds on Cypress Hill, but all they say is one word and that one word is "live," *(Releases scarf and moves to door U. C.)* they say "Live, live, live, live, live!" It's all they've learned, it's the only advice they can give.—Just live…

She opens the door.

Simple!—a very simple instruction.

She goes out U. L. The women's voices rise from the steady, indistinct murmur, like hissing geese.

WOMEN. —No, not liquor! Dope!—Something not normal all right!—Her father and brother were warned by the vigilantes to keep her out of this county.—She's absolutely degraded!—Yes, corrupt!—Corrupt! *(Etc., etc.)*

As if repelled by their hissing voices, Val suddenly rises and goes out of the store U. C. as—Vee Talbott appears on the landing and calls down to him.

VEE. Mr. Xavier! Where is Mr. Xavier?

BEULAH. *(Coming to C.)* Gone, honey.

DOLLY. *(Sitting in shoe chair.)* You might as well face it, Vee. This is one candidate for salvation that you have lost to the opposition.

BEULAH. *(Sitting in chair at table.)* He's gone off to Cypress Hill with the Cutrere girl.

VEE. *(Descending.)* —If some of you older women in Two River County would set a better example there'd be more decent young people!

BEULAH. What was that remark?

VEE. I mean that people who give drinkin' parties an' get so drunk they don't know which is their husband which is somebody else's and people who serve on the altar guild and still play cards on Sundays—

Beulah rises, crosses to Vee at foot of stairs.

BEULAH. Just stop right there! Now I've discovered the source of that dirty gossip!

Dolly rises, crosses to below table C.

VEE. I'm only repeating what I've been told by others. I never been to these parties!

BEULAH. No, and you never will!

DOLLY. You're a public killjoy!

BEULAH. A professional hypocrite!

VEE. I try to build up characters! You and your drinkin' parties are only concerned with tearin' characters down! I'm goin' upstairs, I'm goin' back upstairs!

She rushes upstairs and exits.

BEULAH. Well, I'm glad I said what I said to that woman. I've got no earthly patience with that sort of hypocriticism. *(Picking up plates.)* Dolly, let's put this perishable stuff in the Frigidaire and leave here. I've never been so thoroughly disgusted! *(Shouts.)* Pee Wee!

She goes out R.

DOLLY. Oh, my Lawd. *(Pauses at table and shouts.)* DAWG!

Dolly goes out with the dishes after Beulah.

SISTER. *(Descending stairs.)* Both of those wimmen are as common as dirt.

EVA. *(Following Sister.)* Dolly's folks in Blue Mountain are nothin' at all but the poorest kind of white trash. Why, Lollie Tucker told me the old man sits on the porch with his shoes off drinkin' beer out of a bucket!—Let's take these flowers with us to put on the altar.

Eva takes vase of flowers from table and hands to Sister.

SISTER. Yes, we can give Jabe credit in the parish notes.

EVA. *(Taking plate and jar of olives.)* I'm going to take these olive nut sandwiches, too. They'll come in handy for the bishop adjutant's tea.

Dolly and Beulah cross through from off R. to door U. C.

DOLLY. We still have time to make the second show. *(Shouting.)* DAWG!

BEULAH. *(Shouting.)* Pee Wee!

> *They rush out of store up C.*

SISTER. Sits on the porch with his shoes off?

EVA. Drinkin' beer out of a bucket!

> *Eva and Sister go out U. C. Men (Sheriff Talbott, Pee Wee, Dog) descend stairs.*

TALBOTT. Well, it looks to me like Jabe will more than likely go under before the cotton comes up.

PEE WEE. He never looked good.

DOG. New, but now he looks worse.

> *They cross to door.*

TALBOTT. Where in hell is my wife? VEE!

VEE. *(From landing.)* Hush that bawling. I had to speak to Lady about that boy and I couldn't speak to her in front of Jabe because he thinks he's gonna be able to go back to work himself.

TALBOTT. Well, move along, Mama, quit foolin'!

> *Vee is starting down steps from landing, then stops.*

VEE. I think I ought to wait till that boy gits back.

TALBOTT. I'm sick of you making a damn fool of yourself over every stray bastard that wanders into this county.

> *Sheriff Talbott exits up C. while Vee remains standing on steps until lights fade out. Offstage guitar music fades in. Dog bays in distance as lights dim out to indicate short passage of time. [Sound Cue 3.]*

SCENE 2

The music fades out.

A couple of hours later that night. Through the great window the landscape is faintly luminous under a scudding moonlit sky. Outside a girl's laughter, Carol's, rings out high and clear and is followed by the sound of a motor rapidly going off. [Sound Cue 4.]

Val enters the store u. c. before the car sound quite fades out. He picks up his guitar which he had left above counter. Footsteps descending: Lady appears on the landing in a rayon wrapper, shivering in the cold air. She turns on lamp over counter. She doesn't see Val, who stands behind the shadowy counter, and she goes directly to the phone near the stairs. Her manner is desperate, her voice harsh and shrill.

LADY. Ge' me the drugstore, will you? I know the drugstore's closed, this is Mrs. Torrance, my store's closed, too, but I got a sick man here, just back from the hospital, yeah, yeah, an emergency, well, wake up Mr. Dubinsky, keep ringing till he answers, it's an emergency!

    Pause.

(Mutters under her breath.) —I wish I was dead, dead, dead...

VAL. *(Quietly.)* No, you don't, ma'am.

    She gasps, turning and seeing him. Without leaving the phone, she rings the cashbox open and snatches out something.

LADY. What're you doin' here? You know this store is closed!

VAL. I seen a light was still on and the door was open so I come back to—

LADY. You see what I got in my hand?

    Lady raises revolver above level of counter.

VAL. You going to shoot me?

LADY. I sure will if you don't get out of here, mister!

VAL. That's all right, ma'am, I just come back to pick up my guitar.

LADY. To pick up your guitar?

He lifts it gravely.

—Huh...

VAL. Miss Talbott brought me here. I was here when you got back from Memphis, don't you remember?

LADY. —Aw. Aw, yeah. ...You been here all this time?

VAL. No. I went out and come back.

LADY. *(Into phone.)* I told you to keep ringing till he answers! Go on, keep ringing, keep ringing! *(Then to Val as she puts revolver back in cashbox.)* You went out and come back?

VAL. Yeah.

LADY. What for?

VAL. You know that girl that was here?

LADY. Carol Cutrere?

VAL. She said she had car trouble and could I fix it.

LADY. —Did you fix it?

VAL. She didn't have no car trouble, that wasn't her trouble, oh, she had trouble, all right, but *that* wasn't it...

LADY. What was her trouble?

VAL. She made a mistake about me.

LADY. What mistake?

VAL. She thought I had a sign "Male at Stud" hung on me.

LADY. She thought you—?

Val puts guitar on counter.

(Into phone suddenly.) Oh, Mr. Dubinsky, I'm sorry to wake you up but I just brought my husband back from the Memphis hospital and I left my box of Luminal tablets in the—I got to have some! I ain't slep' for three nights, I'm going to pieces, you hear me. I got to have some tonight. ...Now you look here, if you want to keep my trade, you send me over some tablets. Then bring them yourself, God damn it, excuse my French! Because I'm going to pieces right this minute!

She hangs up violently.

29

—I'm shivering! At night—it's cold as an ice plant in this store. *(Crossing below table.)* Now what do you want? I got to go upstairs.

VAL. Here. Put this on you.

> *He removes his jacket and hands it to her. She doesn't take it at once, stares at him questioningly, and then slowly takes the jacket in her hands and examines it, running her fingers curiously over the snakeskin.*

LADY. What is this stuff this thing's made of? It looks like it was snakeskin.

VAL. Yeah, well, that's what it is.

LADY. What're you doing with a snakeskin jacket?

VAL. It's a sort of a trademark, people call me Snakeskin.

LADY. Who calls you Snakeskin?

VAL. Oh, in the bars, the sort of places I work in—but I've quit that. I'm through with that stuff now...

LADY. You're a—entertainer?

VAL. I sing and play the guitar.

LADY. —Aw?

> *She puts the jacket on as if to explore it.*

It feels warm all right.

VAL. It's warm from my body, I guess...

LADY. You must be a warm-blooded boy...

VAL. That's right...

LADY. Well, what are you lookin' for around here?

VAL. —Work.

LADY. —Boys like you don't work.

VAL. —What d'you mean by boys like me?

LADY. Ones that play th' guitar and go around talkin' about how warm they are...

VAL. That happens t' be the truth. My temperature's always a couple degrees above normal the same as a dog's, it's normal for me the same as it is for a dog, that's the truth...

LADY. —Huh!

VAL. You don't believe me?

LADY. I have no reason to doubt you, but what about it?

VAL. —Why—nothing…

Lady laughs softly and suddenly. Val smiles slowly and warmly.

LADY. You're a peculiar somebody all right, you sure are! How did you get around here?

VAL. I was driving through here last night and an axle broke on my car, and I went to the county jail for a place to sleep out of the rain. Mizz Talbott, Sheriff's wife, took me in and give me a cot in the hoosegow and said if I hung around till you got back that you might give me a job in the store to help out since your husband was tooken sick.

LADY. —Uh-huh. Well—she was wrong about that. …If I took on help here it would have to be local help, I couldn't hire no stranger with a—a snakeskin jacket and a guitar…and that runs a temperature as high as a dog's!

She starts to take off the jacket.

VAL. Keep it on.

LADY. *(Crossing L. to behind counter.)* No, I got to go up now and you had better be going…

VAL. I got nowhere to go.

LADY. Well, everyone's got a problem and that's yours.

VAL. *(Putting jacket on.)* —What nationality are you?

LADY. Why do you ask me that?

VAL. You seem to be like a foreigner.

LADY. I'm the daughter of a Wop bootlegger that was killed here.

VAL. Killed?

LADY. Yeah. The story's well known around here.

Jabe knocks on ceiling.

I got to go up, I'm being called for. That door locks behind you.

She turns out light over counter and starts upstairs, and at the same moment Val begins to sing softly with his guitar, "Heavenly Grass." He suddenly stops short and says abruptly:

VAL. I do electric repairs.

> *Lady stares at him softly.*

I can do all kinds of odd jobs. Ma'am, I'm thirty today and I'm through with the life that I've been leading. I lived in corruption but I'm not corrupted. Here is why. *(Holds up his guitar.)* My life's companion! It washes me clean like water when anything unclean has touched me...

LADY. *(Coming back downstairs.)* What's all that writing on it?

VAL. Autographs of musicians.

LADY. Can I see it?

VAL. Turn on that light above you.

> *She switches on green shaded bulb over counter. Val holds the instrument tenderly between them as if it were a child, his voice soft, intimate, tender.*

See this name? Leadbelly?

LADY. Leadbelly?

VAL. Greatest man ever lived on the twelve-string guitar! Played it so good he broke the stone heart of a Texas governor with it and won himself a pardon out of jail. ...And see this name Oliver? King Oliver? That name is immortal, lady. Greatest man since Gabriel on a horn...

LADY. What's this name?

VAL. Oh. That name? That name is also immortal. The name Bessie Smith is written in the stars!—Jim Crow killed her, John Barley-corn and Jim Crow killed Bessie Smith. She bled to death after an auto accident, because they wouldn't take her into a white hospital... See this name here? That's another immortal!

LADY. Blind Lemon Jefferson? Is his name written in the stars, too?

VAL. Yes, his name is written in the stars, too...

> *Her voice is also intimate and soft: a spell of softness between them, their bodies almost touching, only divided by the guitar.*

LADY. You had any sales experience?

VAL. All my life I been selling something to someone.

LADY. So's everybody. You got any character reference on you?

VAL. I have this—letter.

Val removes a worn, folded letter from a wallet. He passes the letter to her gravely.

LADY. *(Reading slowly aloud.)* "This boy worked for me three months in my auto repair shop and is a real hard worker and is good and honest but is a peculiar talker and that is the reason I got to let him go but would like to— *(Holds letter closer to light.)* keep him. Yours truly."

Val stares at her gravely, blinking a little.

Huh!—Some reference!

VAL. *(Crossing to behind chair c.)* —Is that what it says?

LADY. Didn't you know what it said?

VAL. No, ma'am. He sealed the envelope.

Lady returns letter—crossing to shoe chair D. R.

LADY. Well, that's not the sort of character reference that will do you much good, boy.

VAL. Naw. I guess it ain't.

LADY. —However...

VAL. —What?

LADY. *(Sits in shoe chair.)* What people say about you don't mean much. Can you read shoe sizes?

VAL. I guess so.

LADY. What does 75 David mean?

Val stares at her, shakes head slowly.

75 means seven and one half long and David means "D" wide. Can you count?

VAL. I can count.

LADY. You know how to make change?

VAL. Yeah, I could make change in a store.

LADY. Change for better or worse? Ha ha!—Well—

Pause.

—well—you see that other room there, through that arch there?

She rises—moves U. R. C.

That's the confectionery, it's closed now but it's going to be reopened in a short while and I'm going to compete for the night-life in this county, the after-the-movies trade. I'm going to serve set-ups in there and I'm going to redecorate. I got it all planned. *(Talking eagerly now, as if to herself.)* Artificial branches of fruit trees in flower on the walls and ceilings!—it's going to be like an orchard in the spring!—My father, he had an orchard on Moon Lake. He made a wine garden of it. We had fifteen little white arbors with tables in them and they were covered with—grape vines and—we sold dago red wine an' bootleg whiskey and beer.—They burned it up one summer.

VAL. Who burned it up?

LADY. An outfit in this county called the Mystic Crew rode out there one night with a blowtorch an' gallons of coal oil and set the whole thing on fire, and I want you to know that not a single fire engine in this county pulled out of the station that night. My papa, he took a blanket and run up into the orchard to fight the fire single-handed. He burned alive in it…burned alive! I heard him scream in the orchard—I ran—I fell—I saw him run toward me with his clothes on fire. Whenever I look at a man in this county, I wonder if he was one of 'em that set our orchard on fire!

> *Figure appears at the door U. C., knocks and calls: "Mrs. Torrance?"*

Oh, that's the sandman with my sleeping tablets.

> *She crosses to door U. C.*

Thanks, Mr. Dubinsky, sorry I had to disturb you, sorry I—

> *Man mutters something, hands her the bottle of tablets and goes. She closes the door.*

Well, go to hell, then, old bastard… *(Returns with package.)* —You ever have trouble sleeping?

VAL. I can sleep or not sleep as long or short as I want to.

LADY. Is that right?

VAL. *(Leaning back against counter.)* I can sleep on a concrete floor or go without sleeping, without even feeling sleepy, for forty-eight hours. And I can hold my breath three minutes without blacking out, I made ten dollars betting I could do it and I did it! And I can go a whole day without passing water.

LADY. *(Startled.)* Is that a fact?

VAL. *(Very simply, as if he'd made an ordinary remark.)* That's a fact. I served time on a chain gang for vagrancy once and they tied me to a post all day and I stood there all day without passing water to show the sons of bitches that I could do it.

LADY. —I see what that auto repair man was talking about when he said this boy is a peculiar talker! Well— *(Sitting at table.)* What else can you do? Tell me some more about your self-control!

VAL. *(Grinning.)* Well, they say that a woman can burn a man down. But I can burn down a woman.

LADY. Which woman?

VAL. Any two-footed woman.

> *Lady throws back her head in sudden friendly laughter as he grins at her with the simple candor of a child.*

LADY. —Well, there's lots of two-footed women round here that might be willin' to test the truth of that statement.

VAL. I'm saying I could. I'm not saying I would.

LADY. Don't worry, boy. I'm one two-footed woman that you don't have to convince of your perfect controls.

VAL. No, I'm done with all that.

LADY. What's the matter? Have they tired you out?

VAL. *(Crossing above to D. R.)* I'm not tired. I'm fed up.

LADY. Aw, you're fed up, huh?

VAL. I'm telling you, lady, there's people bought and sold in this world like carcasses of hogs in butcher shops!

LADY. You ain't tellin' me nothin' I don't know.

VAL. You might think there's many and many kinds of people in this world but, lady, there's just two kinds of people, the ones that are bought and the buyers! No!—there's one other kind...

LADY. What kind's that?

VAL. Oh, bums like me with character references that describe them as crazy.

He laughs at himself—sits on shoe stool.

That's some character reference, ha, ha.—You know what I think people mean when they call me crazy?

LADY. What?

VAL. I think they mean I just don't have my two feet on the ground.

LADY. You rise above it?

Offstage guitar music fades in.

VAL. I try to. You know they's a kind of bird that don't have legs so it can't light on nothing but has to stay all its life on its wings in the sky? That's true. I seen one once, it had died and fallen to earth and it was light-blue colored and its body was tiny as your little finger, that's the truth, it had a body as tiny as your little finger and so light on the palm of your hand it didn't weigh more than a feather, but its wings spread out this wide but they was transparent, the color of the sky and you could see through them. That's what they call protection coloring. Camouflage, they call it. You can't tell those birds from the sky and that's why the hawks don't catch them, don't see them up there in the high blue sky near the sun!

LADY. How about in gray weather?

VAL. They fly so high in gray weather the goddam hawks would get dizzy. But those little birds they don't have no legs at all and they live their whole lives on the wing, and they sleep on the wind, that's how they sleep at night, they just spread their wings and go to sleep on the wind like other birds fold their wings and go to sleep on a tree. …They sleep on the wind and… *(His eyes grow soft and vague.)* Never light on this earth but one time when they die!

Music fades out.

LADY. —I'd like to be one of those birds.

VAL. So'd I like to be one of those birds, they's lots of people would like to be one of those birds and never be—corrupted!

LADY. If one of those birds ever dies and falls on the ground and you happen to find it, I wish you would show it to me because I think maybe you just imagine there is a bird of that kind in existence. Because I don't think nothing living has ever been that free, not even nearly. Show me one of them birds and I'll say, "Yes, God's made

36

one perfect creature!"—I sure would give this mercantile store and every bit of stock in it to be that tiny bird the color of the sky...for one night to sleep on the wind and—Float!—around under th'—stars...

Jabe knocks on floor. Lady's eyes return to Val.

—Because I live with a son of a bitch who bought me at a fire sale, and not in fifteen years have I had a single good dream, not one—oh!—Hell...I don't know why I'm—telling a stranger—this...

She draws away from him abruptly and rings the cashbox open.

Take this dollar and go eat at the Al-Nite on the highway and come back here in the morning and I'll put you to work.

Val rises—crosses to counter.

I'll break you in clerking here and when the new confectionery opens, well, maybe I can use you in there. *(Hands him dollar.)* —But let's get one thing straight.

VAL. What thing?

LADY. I'm not interested in your perfect functions, in fact you don't interest me no more than the air that you stand in. If that's understood we'll have a good working relation, but otherwise trouble!—Of course I know you're crazy but they's lots of crazier people than you are still running loose and some of them in high positions, too. Just remember. No monkey business with me. Now go. Go eat, you're hungry.

VAL. Mind if I leave this here? My life's companion?

He means his guitar.

LADY. Leave it here if you want to.

VAL. Thanks, lady.

LADY. Don't mention it.

He crosses toward the u. c. door. He turns to smile back at her and says:

VAL. I don't know nothing about you except you're nice but you are just about the nicest person that I have ever run into! And I'm going to be steady and honest and hard-working to please you and by the way, I can solve your not sleeping problem.

LADY. How?

VAL. A lady osteopath taught me how to make little adjustments in the neck-bone and spine. It will give you a sound natural sleep. Good night!

> *He goes out* U. C. *Count five. Then she throws back her head and laughs as lightly and gaily as a young girl. Then she turns and wonderingly picks up and runs her hands tenderly over his guitar as—*

THE CURTAIN FALLS

ACT II

Scene 1

The store, afternoon, a few weeks later. The table and chair formerly D. C. are back in the confectionery. The shoe-fitting chairs have been moved U. R. in front of R. window. The shoe-boxes have been removed. The chair U. L. has been moved R. of counter, slightly above C. A shawl hangs on hook in window R. of door.

Lady is hanging up the phone. Val is standing just outside the U. C. door. He is wearing a dark blue business suit. He turns and enters. Outside on the highway a mule team is laboring to pull a big truck back on the icy pavement. A Negro's voice shouts: "Hyyyyyyyyy-up." (Twice.) [Sound Cue 5.]

VAL. *(Moving to R. window, looks out.)* One a them big Diamond T trucks an' trailers gone off the highway last night and a six-mule team is tryin' t' pull it back on…

LADY. *(Coming to R. of counter.)* Mister, we just now gotten a big fat complaint about you from a woman that says if she wasn't a widow her husband would come in here and beat the tar out of you.

VAL. *(A step toward her.)* Yeah?—Is this a small pink-headed woman?

LADY. *Pin*-headed woman did you say?

VAL. Naw, I said, "pink"!—A little pink-haired woman, in a checkered coat with pearl buttons this big on it.

LADY. I talked to her on the phone. She didn't go into such details about her appearance but she did say you got familiar. I said, "How? by his talk or behavior?" And she said, "Both!"—Now I was afraid of this when I warned you last week, "No monkey business here, Boy!"

VAL. This little pink-headed woman bought a valentine from me and all I said is my *name* is Valentine to her. Few minutes later a small colored boy come in and delivered the valentine to me with something wrote on it an' I believe I still got it…

39

Val finds and shows it to Lady, who goes to him—Lady reads it, and tears it fiercely to pieces. He lights a cigarette.

LADY. Signed it with a lipstick kiss? You didn't show up for this date?

VAL. No, ma'am. That's why she complained. *(Throws match on floor.)*

LADY. Pick that match up off the floor.

VAL. Are you bucking for sergeant, or something?

He throws match out the u. c. door with elaborate care. She moves back below counter. Her eyes follow his back. Val moves lazily toward her.

LADY. Did you walk around in front of her that way?

VAL. *(At counter.)* What way?

LADY. Slew foot, slew foot!

He regards her closely with good-humored perplexity.

Did you stand in front of her like that? That close? In that, that—*position*?

VAL. What position?

LADY. Ev'rything you do is suggestive!

VAL. Suggestive of what?

LADY. Of what you said you was through with—somethin'—*Oh, shoot, you know what I mean*—Why'd ya think I give you a plain, dark business suit to work in?

VAL. *(Sadly.)* Un-hun...

He sighs and removes his blue jacket.

LADY. Now what're you takin' that off for?

VAL. I'm giving the suit back to you. I'll change my pants in the closet. *(Gives her the jacket and crosses into alcove d. l.)*

LADY. Hey! I'm sorry! You hear me? I didn't sleep well last night. Hey! I said I'm sorry! You hear me?

Lady enters alcove and returns immediately with Val's guitar and crosses to d. r. He follows...

VAL. Le' me have my guitar, Lady. You find too many faults with me and I tried to do good.

LADY. I told you I'm sorry. You want me to get down and lick the dust off your shoes?

VAL. Just give me back my guitar.

LADY. I ain't dissatisfied with you. I'm pleased with you, sincerely!

VAL. You sure don't show it.

LADY. My nerves are all shot to pieces. Shake.

VAL. You mean I ain't fired, so I don't have to quit?

> *They shake hands like two men. She hands him guitar—then silence falls between them.*

LADY. You see, we don't know each other, we're, we're—just gettin'—acquainted.

VAL. That's right, like a couple of animals sniffin' around each other...

> *The image embarrasses her. He crosses to counter, leans over and puts guitar behind it.*

LADY. Well, not exactly like *that*, but—!

VAL. We don't know each other. How do people get to know each other? I used to think they did it by touch.

LADY. By what?

VAL. By touch, by touchin' each other.

LADY. *(Moving up and sitting on shoe-fitting chair which has been moved to R. window.)* Oh, you mean by close—contact!

VAL. But later it seemed like that made them more strangers than ever, uh-huh, more strangers than ever...

LADY. Then how d'you think they get to know each other?

VAL. *(Sitting on counter.)* Well, in answer to your question, I would say this. Nobody ever gets to know *nobody!* We're all of us sentenced to solitary confinement inside our own skins, for life! You understand me, Lady?—I'm tellin' you it's the truth, we got to face it, we're under a lifelong sentence to solitary confinement inside our own lonely skins for as long as we live on this earth!

LADY. *(Rises—crossing to him.)* Oh, no, I'm not a big optimist but I cannot agree with something as sad as that statement!

> *They are sweetly grave as two children: the store is somewhat dusky. She sits in chair R. of counter.*

VAL. *Listen!*—When I was a kid on Witches Bayou? After my folks all scattered away like loose chicken's feathers blown around by the wind?—I stayed there alone on the bayou, hunted and trapped out of season and hid from the law!—*Listen!*—All that time, all that lonely time, I felt I was—waiting for something!

LADY. What for?

VAL. What does anyone wait for? For something to happen, for anything to happen, to make things make more sense. ...It's hard to remember what that feeling was like because I've lost it now, but I was waiting for something like if you ask a question you wait for someone to answer, but you ask the wrong question or you ask the wrong person and the answer don't come. Does everything stop because you don't get the answer? No, it goes right on as if the answer was given, day comes after day and night comes after night, and you're still waiting for someone to answer the question and going right on as if the question was answered. And then—well—then...

LADY. Then what?

VAL. You get the make-believe answer.

LADY. What answer is that?

VAL. Don't pretend you don't know because you do!

LADY. —Love?

VAL. *(Places hand on her shoulder.)* That's the make-believe answer, it's fooled many a fool besides you an' me, that's the God's truth, Lady, and you had better believe it.

> Lady looks reflectively at Val and he goes on speaking and sits on stool below counter.

—I met a girl on the bayou when I was fourteen. I'd had a feeling that day that if I just kept poling the boat down the bayou a little bit further I would come bang into whatever it was I'd been so long expecting!

LADY. Was she the answer, this girl that you met on the bayou?

VAL. She made me think that she was.

LADY. How did she do that?

VAL. By coming out on the dog-trot of a cabin as naked as I was in that flat-bottom boat! She stood there a while with the daylight blazing around her as bright as heaven as far as I could see. You seen the inside of a shell, how white that is, pearly white? Her naked skin was like that.—Oh, God, I remember a bird flown out of the moss and its wings made a shadow on her, and then it sung a single, high clear note, and as if she was waiting for that as a kind of a signal to catch me, she turned and smiled, and walked on back in the cabin…

LADY. You followed?

VAL. Yes, I followed, I followed, like a bird's tail follows a bird, I followed! I thought that she give me the answer to the question I'd been waiting for, but afterwards I wasn't sure that was it, but from that time the question wasn't much plainer than the answer and—

LADY. —What?

VAL. At fifteen I left Witches Bayou. My dog died, I sold my boat and the gun… I went to New Orleans in that snakeskin jacket… It didn't take long for me to learn the score.

LADY. What did you learn?

VAL. I learned that I had something to sell besides snakeskin and other wild things' skins I caught on the bayou. I was corrupted! That's the answer…

LADY. Naw, that ain't the answer!

VAL. Okay, *you* tell me the answer!

LADY. I don't know the answer, I just know corruption ain't the answer. I know that much. If I thought that was the answer I'd take Jabe's pistol or his morphine tablets and—

A woman bursts into store U. C.

WOMAN. I got to use your pay phone!

Sound of car horn off L. [Sound Cue 6.]

LADY. Go ahead. Help yourself.

Woman crosses to phone, deposits coin. Lady crosses to confectionery.

(To Val.) Get me a Coke from the cooler.

Val crosses and goes out R.

During the intense activity among the choral women, Lady and Val seem bemused, as if they were thinking back over their talk before. For the past few moments a car horn has been heard blowing repeatedly in the near distance. *[Sound Cue 6 repeated.]*

WOMAN. *(At phone.)* Cutrere Place, get me the Cutrere Place, will yuh? David Cutrere or his wife whichever comes to the phone!

Car horn fades out. Beulah rushes in U. C. from the street, goes R. C.

BEULAH. Lady, lady, where's Lady! Carol Cutrere is—!

WOMAN. Quiet, please! I am callin' her brother about her!

Lady sits at table in confectionery.

(At phone.) Who's this I'm talking to? Good! I'm calling about your sister, Carol Cutrere. She is blowing her car horn at the Red Crown station, she is blowing and blowing her car horn at the Red Crown station because my husband give the station attendants instructions not to service her car, and she is blowing and blowing and blowing on her horn, drawing a big crowd there. And, Mr. Cutrere, I thought that you and your father had agreed to keep that girl out of Two River County for good, that's what we all understood around here.

Car horn again off L. [Sound Cue 6 repeated.]

BEULAH. *(Listening with excited approval.)* Good! Good! Tell him that if—

Dolly enters up C.

DOLLY. She's gotten out of the car and—

BEULAH. *Shhh!*

WOMAN. *(At phone.)* Well, I just wanted to let you know she's back here in town makin' another disturbance and my husband's on the phone now at the Red Crown Station—

Beulah goes outside and looks off.

—trying to get the sheriff, so if she gits picked up again by th' law, you can't say I didn't warn you, Mr. Cutrere.

Car horn.

DOLLY. *Oh, good! Good!*

BEULAH. *(Coming back in.)* Where is she, where's she gone now?

WOMAN. *(At phone.)* You better be quick about it. Yes, I do. I sympathize with you and *your* father and with Mrs. Cutrere but

Carol cannot demand service at our station, we just refuse to wait on her, she's not—Hello? Hello?

> *She jiggles phone violently.*

BEULAH. What's he doin'? Comin' to pick her up?

DOLLY. Call the sheriff's office!

> *Beulah goes outside again. Val comes back from R. with a bottle of Coca-Cola—hands it to Lady and leans on jukebox.*

(Going out to Beulah.) What's goin' on now?

BEULAH. *(Outside.)* Look, look, they're pushing her out of the station driveway.

> *They forget Lady in this new excitement. Ad libs continual. The woman from the station charges back out of the store.*

DOLLY. Where is Carol?

BEULAH. Going into the White Star Pharmacy!

> *Dolly rushes back to the phone.*

(Coming back in; to Lady.) Lady, I want you to give me your word that if that Cutrere girl comes in here, you won't wait on her! You hear me?

LADY. No.

BEULAH. —What? Will you refuse to wait on her?

LADY. I can't refuse to wait on anyone in this store.

BEULAH. Well, I'd like to know why you can't.

DOLLY. Shhh! I'm on the phone!

BEULAH. Who you phonin', Dolly?

DOLLY. That White Star Pharmacy! I want to make sure that Mr. Dubinsky refuses to wait on that girl! *(Having found and deposited coin.)* I want the White Far Starmacy. I mean the— *(Stamps foot.)* White Star Pharmacy!—I'm so upset my tongue's twisted!

> *Lady hands Coke to Val. Beulah is at the window.*

I'm getting a busy signal. Has she come out yet?

BEULAH. No, she's still in the White Star!

DOLLY. Maybe they're not waiting on her.

BEULAH. Dubinsky'd wait on a purple-bottom baboon if it put a dime on th' counter an' pointed at something!

45

DOLLY. I know she sat at a table in the Blue Bird Cafe half'n hour last time she was here and the waitresses never come near her!

BEULAH. That's different. They're not foreigners there! *(Crosses to counter; this is meant for Dolly.)* You can't ostracize a person out of this county unless everybody cooperates. Lady just told me that she was going to wait on her if she comes here.

DOLLY. Lady wouldn't do that.

BEULAH. *Ask* her! She told *me* she would!

> *Lady rises and turns at once to the women and shouts at them—*

LADY. Oh, for God's sake, no! I'm not going to refuse to wait on her because you all don't like her! Besides I'm delighted that wild girl is givin' her brother so much trouble!

> *After this outburst she crosses L. to back of the counter.*

DOLLY. *(At phone.)* Hush! Mr. Dubinsky! This is Dolly Hamma, Mr. Dog Hamma's wife!

> *Carol quietly enters the front door U. C. She wears the trenchcoat.*

I want to ask you, is Carol Cutrere in your drugstore?

BEULAH. *(Warningly.)* Dolly!

CAROL. No. She isn't.

DOLLY. —What?

CAROL. She's here.

> *Beulah goes into confectionery and sits on chair. Carol moves toward Val to D. R. C.*

DOLLY. —Aw!—Never mind, Mr. Dubinsky.

> *Dolly hangs up furiously and crosses to door. A silence in which they all stare at the girl from various positions about the store. She has been on the road all night in an open car: her hair is blown wild, her face flushed and eyes bright with fever. Her manner in the scene is that of a wild animal at bay, desperate but fearless.*

LADY. *(Finally and quietly.)* Hello, Carol.

CAROL. Hello, Lady.

LADY. *(Defiantly cordial.)* I thought that you were in New Orleans, Carol.

46

CAROL. Yes, I was. Last night.

LADY. Well, you got back fast.

CAROL. I drove all night.

LADY. In that storm?

CAROL. The wind took the top off my car but I didn't stop.

>*She watches Val steadily, he steadily ignores her—turns away and puts bottle of Coca-Cola on a table.*

LADY. *(With growing impatience.)* Is something wrong at home, is someone sick?

CAROL. *(Absently.)* No. No, not that I know of, I wouldn't know if they were, they—May I sit down?

LADY. Why, sure.

CAROL. *(Crossing to chair R. of counter and sits.)* —They pay me to stay away so I wouldn't know...

>*Silence. Val walks deliberately past her and goes into alcove.*

—I think I have a fever, I feel like I'm catching pneumonia, everything's so far away...

>*Silence again except for the faint, hissing whispers of Beulah and Dolly at the back of the store.*

LADY. *(With a touch of exasperation.)* Is there something you want?

CAROL. Everything seems miles away...

LADY. Carol, I said is there anything you want here?

CAROL. Excuse me!—yes...

LADY. Yes, what?

CAROL. Don't bother now. I'll wait.

>*Val comes out of alcove with the blue jacket on.*

LADY. Wait for what, what are you waiting for! You don't have to wait for nothing, just say what you want and if I got it in stock I'll give it to you!

>*Phone rings once.*

CAROL. *(Vaguely.)* —Thank you—no...

LADY. *(To Val.)* Get that phone, Val.

>*Lady gets a pint bottle and glass and pours a drink for Carol*

47

and puts bottle back under counter. Dolly crosses and hisses something inaudible to Beulah.

BEULAH. *(Rising.)* I just want to wait here to see if she does or she don't.

DOLLY. She just said she would!

BEULAH. Just the same, I'm gonna wait!!

VAL. *(At phone.)* Yes, sir, she is—I'll tell her. *(Hangs up and speaks to Lady.)* Her brother's heard she's here and he's coming to pick her up.

LADY. *David Cutrere is not coming in this store!*

DOLLY. Aw-aw!

BEULAH. David Cutrere used to be her lover.

DOLLY. I remember you told me.

LADY. *(Wheels about suddenly toward the women.)* Beulah! Dolly! Why're you back there hissing together like geese? *(Coming from behind counter to R. C.)* Why don't you go to th'—Blue Bird and—have some hot coffee—talk there!

BEULAH. Well! It looks like we're getting what they call the bum's rush.

DOLLY. I never stay where I'm not wanted and when I'm not wanted somewhere I never come back!

They cross out and slam door up c.

LADY. *(After a pause.)* What did you come here for?

CAROL. To deliver a message.

LADY. To me?

CAROL. No.

LADY. Then who?

Carol stares at Lady gravely a moment, then turns slowly to look at Val.

—Him?—Him?

Carol nods slowly and slightly.

OK, then, give him the message, deliver the message to him.

CAROL. It's a private message. Could I speak to him alone, please?

Lady gets a shawl from a hook in window R. of U. C. door.

48

LADY. Oh, for God's sake! Your brother's plantation is ten minutes from here in that sky-blue Cadillac his rich wife give him. Now look. He's on his way here but I won't let him come in, I don't even want his hand to touch the door handle. I know your message, this boy knows your message, there's nothing private about it. But I tell you that this boy's not for sale in my store!—Now.—I'm going out to watch for the sky-blue Cadillac on the highway. When I see it, I'm going to throw this door open and holler and when I holler, I want you out of this door like a shot from a pistol!—that fast! Understand?

> *Lady slams U. C. door behind her. The loud noise of the door slam increases the silence that follows. Val's oblivious attitude is not exactly hostile, but deliberate. There's a kind of purity in it: also a kind of refusal to concern himself with a problem that isn't his own. He holds his guitar with a specially tender concentration, and strikes a soft chord on it. The girl stares at Val. Val sits on downstage edge of counter, one foot up on stool.*
>
> *Since this scene is followed by the emotional scene between Lady and David, it should be keyed somewhat lower than written; it's important that Val should not seem brutal in his attitude toward Carol, there should be an air between them of two lonely children.*

VAL. *(In a soft preoccupied tone.)* You told the lady I work for that you had a message for me. Is that right, miss? Have you got a message for me?

> *Carol rises, moves a few steps toward him, hesitantly.*

CAROL. You've spilt some ashes on your new blue suit.

> *She brushes the sleeve of his jacket with light, lingering fingers.*

VAL. Is that the message?

CAROL. *(Moves away a step.)* No. No, that was just an excuse to touch you. The message is—

VAL. What?

> *Offstage guitar music fades in.*

CAROL. —I'd love to hold something the way you hold your guitar, that's how I'd love to hold something, with such—*tender protection!* I'd love to hold *you* that way, with that same—*Tender Protection!*

Her hand has fallen onto his knee, which he has drawn up to rest a foot on the counter stool.

—Because you hang the moon for me!

He puts guitar down and goes to her. He speaks to her, not roughly but in a tone that holds a long history that began with a romantic acceptance of such declarations as she has just made to him, and that burned gradually to his present distrust.

VAL. Who're you tryin' t' fool beside you'self? You couldn't stand the weight of a man's body on you.

He casually picks up her wrist and pushes the sleeve back from it.

What's this here? A human wrist with a bone? It feels like a twig I could snap with two fingers...

Gently, negligently, he pushes collar of her trenchcoat back from her bare throat and shoulders. Runs a finger along her neck, tracing a vein.

Little girl, you're transparent, I can see the veins in you. A man's weight on you would break you like a bundle of sticks...

Music fades out.

CAROL. *(Gazes at him, startled by his perception.)* Isn't it funny! You've hit on the truth about me. The act of love-making is almost unbearably painful, and yet, of course, I do bear it, because to be not alone, even for a few moments, is worth the pain and the danger. It's dangerous for me because I'm not built for childbearing.

VAL. Well, then, fly away, little bird, fly away before you—get broke.

He turns back to his guitar.

CAROL. Why do you dislike me?

VAL. *(Turns back.)* I never dislike nobody till they interfere with me.

CAROL. How have I interfered with you? Did I snitch when I saw my cousin's watch on you?

Offstage guitar music fades in.

VAL. *(Beginning to remove his watch.)* —You won't take my word for a true thing I told you. I'm thirty years old and I'm done with the crowd you run with and the places you run to. The Club Rendezvous, the Starlite Lounge, the Music Bar, and all of them all night places. Here— *(Offers watch.)* take this Rolex chronometer that tells the time of the day and the day of the week and the month and all the crazy moon's phases. I never stole nothing before. When I stole that I known it was time for me to get off the party, so take it back, now, to Bertie...

He takes her hand and tries to force the watch into her fist. There is a little struggle, he can't open her fist. She is crying, but staring fiercely into his eyes. He draws a hissing breath and hurls watch violently across the floor.

—That's my message to you and the pack you run with!

CAROL. *(Flings coat away.)* I RUN WITH NOBODY!—I hoped I could run with you...

Music stops short.

You're in danger here, Snakeskin. You've taken off the jacket that said: "I'm wild, I'm alone!" and put on the nice blue uniform of a convict!... Last night I woke up thinking about you again. I drove all night to bring you this warning of danger...

Her trembling hand covers her lips.

—The message I came here to give you was a warning of danger; I hoped you'd hear me and let me take you away before it's—too late.

Door U. C. bursts open. Lady rushes inside, crying out—

LADY. *Your brother's coming, go out! He can't come in!*

Carol picks up coat—goes into confectionery, sobbing.

Lock that door! Don't let him come in my store!

She runs up to the landing of the stairs as Val crosses to U. C. door, but before he can close it David Cutrere appears in doorway. He is a tall man in hunter's clothes. He is hardly less handsome now than he was in his youth, but something has gone: his power is that of a captive who rules over other captives. His face, his eyes, have something of the same desperate, unnatural hardness that Lady meets the world with.

DAVID. Carol?

VAL. She's in there.

He nods toward the dim confectionery R., into which the girl has retreated.

DAVID. *(Crossing.)* Carol!

> *Carol rises and advances a few steps into the lighted area of the stage.*

You broke the agreement.

> *Carol nods slightly, staring at Val.*

(Harshly.) All right. I'll drive you back. Where's your coat?

> *Carol murmurs something inaudible and crosses to Val.*

Where is her coat, where is my sister's coat?

> *Val crosses below and picks up the coat that Carol has dropped on the floor and hands it to David. He throws it roughly about Carol's shoulders and propels her forcefully toward the store entrance up C. Val moves away to D. R.*

LADY. *(Suddenly and sharply.)* Wait, please!

> *David looks up at the landing, stands frozen as Lady walks slowly down the stairs.*

DAVID. *(Softly, hoarsely.)* How—are you, Lady?

LADY. *(Turns to Val.)* Val, go out.

DAVID. *(To Carol.)* Carol, will you wait for me in my car?

> *He opens the door for his sister, she glances back at Val with desolation in her eyes. Val crosses quickly through the confectionery. Carol nods slightly, as if in sad response to some painful question, and goes out of the store U. C. Pause.*

LADY. I told you once to never come in this store.

DAVID. I came for my sister...

> *He turns as if to go.*

LADY. No, wait!

DAVID. I don't dare leave my sister alone on the road.

LADY. I have something to tell you I never told you before.

> *She crosses to him. David turns back to her—then moves away to D. R. C.*

—I—carried your child in my body the summer you quit me.

> *Silence.*

DAVID. —I—didn't know.

52

LADY. No, no, I didn't write you no letter about it, I was proud then, I had pride. But I had your child in my body the summer you quit me, that summer they burned my father in his wine garden, and you, you washed your hands clean of any connection with a dago bootlegger's daughter and—

> *Her breathless voice momentarily falters and she makes a fierce gesture as she struggles to speak.*

—took that—society girl that—restored your homeplace and give you such— *(Catches breath.)* well-born children...

DAVID. —I—didn't know.

LADY. Well, now you do know, you know now. I carried your child in my body the summer you quit me but I had it cut out of my body, and they cut my heart out with it!

DAVID. —I—didn't know.

LADY. I wanted death after that, but death don't come when you want it, it comes when you don't want it! I wanted death, then, but I took the next best thing. You sold yourself. I sold myself. *You* was bought. *I* was bought. You made whores of us both!

DAVID. —I—didn't know...

> *Offstage mandolin music is heard: barely audible.*

LADY. But that's all a long time ago. Some reason I drove by there a few nights ago; the shore of the lake where my father had his wine garden? You remember? You remember the wine garden of my father?

> *David stares at her. She turns away.*

No, you don't? You don't remember it even?

DAVID. —Lady, I don't—remember—anything else...

LADY. The mandolin of my father, the songs that I sang with my father in my father's wine garden?

DAVID. Yes, I don't remember anything else...

LADY. Core Ingrata! Come Le Rose! And we disappeared and he would call, "*Lady? Lady?*" *(Turns to him.) How could I answer him with two tongues in my mouth!*

> *A sharp hissing intake of breath, eyes opened wide, hand clapped over her mouth as if what she said was unendurable*

to her. He turns instantly, sharply away. Music stops short. Jabe begins to knock for her on the floor above. She crosses to stairs—stops—turns.

I hold hard feelings!—Don't ever come here again. If your wild sister comes here, send somebody else for her, not you, not you. Because I hope never to feel this knife again in me.

Her hand is on her chest; she breathes with difficulty. He turns away from her, starts toward the u. c. door and opens it. She takes a step toward him.

And don't pity me neither. I haven't gone down so terribly far in the world. I got a going concern in this mercantile store, in there's the confectionery which'll reopen this spring, it's being done over to make it the place that all the young people will come to, it's going to be like—the wine garden of my father those wine drinking nights when you had something better than anything you've had since!

DAVID. Lady—*that's*—

LADY. —What?

DAVID. —*True!*

LADY. Go now. I just wanted to tell you my life ain't over.

He goes out u. c. as Jabe continues knocking. She stands, stunned, motionless, till Val quietly reenters the store d. r. She becomes aware of his return rather slowly, then she murmurs—

I made a fool of myself…

VAL. What?

LADY. *(Crosses to stairs.)* I made a fool of myself!

She goes up the stairs with effort as the lights change slowly to mark a division of scenes. Val crosses to counter to get his guitar.

Sunset of that day. The sunset is fiery. A large woman opens the door and stands there looking dazed. Vee Talbott. She carries a picture, wrapped in paper.

VAL. *(Turns.)* Hello, Mrs. Talbott.

VEE. Something's gone wrong with my eyes. I can't see nothing.

VAL. *(Goes to her.)* Here, let me help you. You probably drove up here with that setting sun in your face. *(Leading her to shoe-fitting chair at* R. *window.)* There now. Set down right here.

VEE. Thank you—so—much...

VAL. I haven't seen you since that night you brought me here to ask for this job.

VEE. Has the minister called on you yet? Reverend Tooker? I made him promise he would. I told him you were new around here and weren't affiliated to any church yet. I want you to go to ours.

VAL. —That's—mighty—kind of you.

VEE. The Church of the Resurrection, it's Episcopal.

VAL. Uh-huh.

VEE. Unwrap that picture, please.

VAL. Sure.

> *Val tears paper off canvas.*

VEE. It's the Church of the Resurrection. I give it a sort of imaginative treatment. You know, Jabe and Lady have never darkened a church door. I thought it ought to be hung where Jabe could look at it, it might help to bring that poor dying man to Jesus...

> *Val places it against chair* R. *of counter and crouches before the canvas, studying it long and seriously. Val smiles at Vee warmly, then back to the canvas.*

VAL. *(At last.)* What's this here in the picture?

VEE. The steeple.

VAL. Aw.—Is the church steeple red?

VEE. Why—no, but—

VAL. Why'd you paint it red, then?

VEE. Oh, well, you see, I— *(Laughs nervously, child-like in her growing excitement.)* I just, just *felt* it that way! I paint a thing how I feel it instead of always the way it actually is. Appearances are misleading, nothing is what it looks like to the eyes. You got to have—*vision*—to see!

VAL. *(Rises, nodding gravely, emphatically.)* —Yes. Vision. Vision!— to see...

VEE. I paint from vision. They call me a Visionary.

55

VAL. Oh.

VEE. *(With shy pride.)* That's what the New Orleans and Memphis newspaper people admire so much in my work. They call it a primitive style, the work of a Visionary. One of my pictures is hung on the exhibition in Audubon Park museum and they have asked for others. I can't turn them out fast enough!—I have to wait for—visions, no, I—I can't paint without—visions... I couldn't *live* without visions!

VAL. Have you always had visions?

VEE. No, just since I was born, I—!

> *She stops short, startled by the absurdity of her answer. Both laugh suddenly, then she rushes on, her great bosom heaving with curious excitement, twisting in her chair, gesturing with clenched hands.*

I was born, I was born with a caul! A sort of thing like a veil, a thin, thin sort of a web was over my eyes. They call that a caul. It's a sign that you're going to have visions, and I did, I had them!

> *Vee moves to R. and motions to Val to sit next to her, which he does. Pauses for breath. Light fades.*

—When I was little my baby sister died. Just one day old, she died. They had to baptize her at midnight to save her soul.

VAL. Uh-huh.

VEE. The minister came at midnight, and after the baptism service, he handed the bowl of holy water to me and told me, "Be sure to empty this out on the ground!"—I didn't. I was scared to go out at midnight, with, with—death! in the—house and—I sneaked into the kitchen, I emptied the holy water into the kitchen sink—thunder! struck!—the kitchen sink turned black, the kitchen sink turned absolutely black!

> *Sheriff Talbott enters the front door U. C.*

TALBOTT. Mama! What're you doin'?

VEE. Talkin'.

TALBOTT. I'm gonna see Jabe a minute, you go out and wait in th' car.

> *Talbott goes up the stairs. Vee rises slowly—picks up canvas and moves to counter.*

VEE. —Oh, I—tell you!—since I got into this painting, my whole outlook is different. I can't explain how it is, the difference to me.

VAL. You don't have to explain. I know what you mean. Before you started to paint, it didn't make sense.

VEE. —What—what didn't?

VAL. Existence!

VEE. *(Slowly and softly.)* No—no, it didn't. …Existence didn't make sense…

> *She places canvas on guitar on counter and sits in chair by counter.*

VAL. *(Rises—crossing to her.)* You lived in Two River County, the wife of the county sheriff. You saw awful things take place.

VEE. Awful! Things!

VAL. Beatings!

VEE. Yes!

VAL. Lynchings!

VEE. Yes!

VAL. Runaway convicts torn to pieces by hounds!

> *This is the first time she could express this horror. The lights are fading slowly.*

VEE. *Chain-gang dogs!* Tear fugitives to *pieces*!

> *She had half risen, now sinks back faintly. Val looks beyond her in the dim store, his light eyes have a dark gaze. It may be that his speech is too articulate: counteract this effect by groping, hesitations.*

VAL. *(Moves away a step.)* But violence ain't quick always. Sometimes it's slow. Some tornadoes are slow. Corruption—rots men's hearts and—rot is slow…

VEE. —How do you—?

VAL. Know? I been a witness, I know!

VEE. *I* been a witness! *I* know!

VAL. We seen these things from seats down front at th' show.

> *He crouches before her and touches her hands in her lap. Her breath shudders.*

And so you begun to paint your visions. Without no plan, no training, you started to paint as if God touched your fingers.

He lifts her hands slowly, gently from her soft lap.

You made some beauty out of this Two River County with these two woman's hands...

Talbott appears on the stair landing, looks down, silent.

Yeah, you made some beauty!

Strangely, gently, he lifts her hands to his mouth. She gasps. Talbott calls out—

TALBOTT. *Hey!*

Vee springs up, gasping.

(Descending.) Cut this crap!

Val moves away to R. C.

(To Vee.) Go out. Wait in the car.

He stares at Val till Vee lumbers out U. C. as if dazed.

(After a while.) Jabe Torrance told me to take a good look at you. *(Crossing to Val.)* Well, now, I've taken that look.

Nods shortly. Goes out of store U. C. The store is now very dim. As door closes on Talbott, Val picks up painting—goes behind counter and places it on a shelf, then picks up his guitar, sits on counter.

Lights go down to mark a division as he sings and plays "Heavenly Grass." As he finishes song, Lady descends stairs; he rises and turns on green-shaded lightbulb above counter.

VAL. *(To Lady.)* You been up there a long time.

LADY. —I gave him morphine. He must be out of his mind. He says such awful things to me. He says I want him to die.

VAL. You sure you don't?

LADY. I don't want no one to die. Death's terrible, Val.

Pause. She wanders to the front window R. He takes his guitar and crosses to the door.

You gotta go now?

VAL. I'm late.

LADY. Late for what? You got a date with somebody?

VAL. —No…

LADY. Then stay a while. Play something. I'm all unstrung…

> *He crosses back and leans against counter; the guitar is barely audible under the speeches.*

I made a terrible fool of myself down here today with—

VAL. —That girl's brother?

LADY. Yes, I—threw away—pride…

VAL. His sister said she'd come here to give me a warning. I wonder what of?

LADY. *(Sitting in shoe-fitting chair.)* —I said things to him I should of been too proud to say…

> *Each is pursuing his own reflections.*

VAL. Once or twice lately I've woke up with a fast heart, shouting something, and had to pick up my guitar to calm myself down… Somehow or other I can't get used to this place, I don't feel safe in this place, but I—want to stay…

> *Val stops short: sound of wild baying of dogs off up R. [Sound Cue 7, continuing.]*

LADY. The chain-gang dogs are chasing some runaway convict…

VAL. *(Thrusting guitar under his arm, crosses to door U. C.) Run, boy! Run fast, brother! If they catch you, you never will run again! That's—* for sure…

> *The baying of the dogs changes, becomes almost a single savage note.*

—uh-huh—the dogs've got him…

> *Pause.*

They're tearing him to pieces!

> *Pause. Baying continues. Two shots are fired. The baying dies out. Val stops with his hand on the door. [Sound Cue 7 ends.]*

LADY. *Wait!*

VAL. —Huh?

LADY. —Where do you stay?

VAL. —When?

LADY. Nights.

VAL. I stay at the Wildwood cabins on the highway.

LADY. You like it there?

VAL. Uh-huh.

LADY. —Why?

VAL. I got a comfortable bed, a two-burner stove, a shower and icebox there.

LADY. You want to save money?

VAL. I never could in my life.

LADY. You could if you stayed on the place.

VAL. What place?

LADY. This place.

VAL. Whereabouts on this place?

LADY. *(Points to alcove.)* Back of that curtain.

VAL. —Where they try on clothes?

LADY. There's a cot there. A nurse slept on it when Jabe had his first operation, and there's a washroom down here and I'll get a plumber to put in a hot an' cold shower! I'll—fix it up nice for you...

> She rises, crosses to foot of stairs. Pause.

VAL. *(Moving D. C.)* —I—don't like to be—obligated.

LADY. There wouldn't be no obligation, you'd do me a favor. I'd feel safer at night with somebody on the place. I would, it would cost you nothing! And you could save up that money you spend on the cabin. How much? Ten a week? Why, two or three months from now you'd—save enough money to— *(Makes a wide gesture with a short laugh as if startled.)* Go on! Take a look at it! See if it don't suit you!—All right...

> But he doesn't move, he appears reflective.

(Shivering, hugging herself.) Where does heat go in this building?

VAL. *(Reflectively.)* —heat rises...

LADY. You with your dog's temperature, don't feel cold, do you? I do! I turn blue with it!

> The wait is unendurable to Lady.

Well, aren't you going to look at it, the room back there, and see if it suits you or not?!

VAL. —I'll go and take a look at it...

> *He crosses to the alcove and disappears behind the curtain. A light goes on behind it, making a bizarre pattern of it translucent. Lady takes out a pint bottle and a glass from under the counter, setting them down. She pours a drink and sits in chair R. of counter. The lights turn off behind the alcove curtain and Val comes back out. She sits stiffly without looking at him as he crosses back lazily, goes behind counter, puts guitar down. His manner is gently sad, as if he had met with a familiar, expected disappointment. He sits down quietly on edge of counter and takes the pint bottle and pours himself a shot of the liquor with a reflective sigh. Lady's voice is harsh and sudden, demanding—*

LADY. *Well, is it okay or—? What!*

VAL. I never been in a position where I could turn down something I got for nothing in my life. I like that picture in there. That's a famous picture, that *September Morn* picture you got on the wall in there. Ha ha! I might have trouble sleeping in a room with that picture. I might keep turning the light on to take another look at it! The way she's cold in that water and sort of crouched over in it, holding her body like that, that—might—ha ha!—sort of keep me awake...

LADY. You with your perfect control of your functions, it would take more than a picture to keep you awake!

VAL. I was just kidding.

LADY. I was just kidding too.

VAL. But you know how a single man is. He don't come home every night with just his shadow.

> *Pause. She takes a drink.*

LADY. You bring girls home nights to the Wildwood cabins, do you?

VAL. I ain't so far. But I would like to feel free to. That old life is what I'm used to. I always worked nights in cities and if you work nights in cities you live in a different city from those that work days.

LADY. Yes. I know, I—imagine...

VAL. The ones that work days in cities and the ones that work nights in cities, they live in different cities. The cities have the same name but they are different cities. As different as night and day. There's something wild in the country that only the night people know...

LADY. Yeah, I know!

VAL. I'm thirty years old!—but sudden changes don't work, it takes—

LADY. —Time—yes...

> *Slight pause which she finds disconcerting. He slides off counter and moves around below it.*

VAL. You been good to me, Lady.—Why d'you want me to stay here?

LADY. *(Defensively.)* I told you why.

VAL. For company nights?

LADY. Yeah, to, to!—*guard the store*, nights!

VAL. To be a night watchman?

LADY. Yeah, to be a night *watchman.*

VAL. You feel nervous alone here?

LADY. Naturally now!—Jabe sleeps with a pistol next to him but if somebody broke in the store, he couldn't git up and all I could do is holler!—Who'd *hear* me? They got a telephone girl on the night shift with—sleepin' sickness, I think! Anyhow, why're you so suspicious? You look at me like you thought I was *plottin'* somethin'.—Kind people *exist*: Even me!

> *She sits up rigid in chair, lips and eyes tight closed, drawing in a loud breath which comes from a tension both personal and vicarious.*

VAL. I understand, Lady, but... Why're you sitting up so stiff in that chair?

LADY. Ha! *(Sharp laugh, leans back in chair.)*

VAL. You're still unrelaxed.

LADY. I know.

VAL. Relax. *(Moving around close to her.)* I'm going to show you some tricks I learned from a lady osteopath that took me in, too.

LADY. What tricks?

VAL. How to manipulate joints and bones in a way that makes you feel like a loose piece of string.

She watches him.

Do you trust me or don't you?

LADY. Yeah, I trust you completely, but—

VAL. Well then, lean forward a little and raise your arms up and turn sideways in the chair.

She follows those instructions.

Drop your head.

He manipulates her head and neck.

Now the spine, Lady.

He places his knee against the small of her backbone and she utters a sharp, startled laugh as he draws her backbone hard against his kneecap.

LADY. Ha, ha!—That makes a sound like, like, like!—boards contracting with cold in the building, ha, ha!

He relaxes.

VAL. Better?

LADY. Oh, yes!—much...thanks...

VAL. *(Strokes her neck.)* Your skin is like silk. You're light-skinned to be Italian.

LADY. Most people in this country think Italian people are dark. Some are but not all are! Some of them are fair...very fair. ...My father's people were dark but my mother's people were fair. Ha ha!

The laughter is senseless. He smiles understandingly at her as she chatters to cover confusion. He turns away—then goes above and sits on counter close to her.

My mother's mother's sister—come here from Monte Cassino, to die, with relations!—but I think people always die alone...with or without relations. I was a little girl then and I remember it took her such a long, long time to die we almost forgot her.—She was so quiet...in a corner...and I remember asking her one time, "Zia Teresa, how does it feel to die?"—Only a little girl would ask such a question, ha ha! Oh and I remember her answer. She said—"It's a lonely feeling." I think she wished she had stayed in Italy and died in a place that she knew...

> *Lady looks at him directly for the first time since mentioning the alcove.*

Well, there is a washroom, and I'll get the plumber to put in a hot and cold shower!

> *She rises, retreats awkwardly from the chair. His interest seems to have wandered from her.*

I'll go up and get some clean linen and make up that bed in there.

> *She turns and walks rapidly, almost running, to stairs. He appears lost in some private reflection, but as soon as she has disappeared above the landing, he says something under his breath and crosses directly to the cashbox. Coughs loudly to cover the sound of ringing it open. Scoops out a fistful of bills and coughs again to cover the sound of slamming drawer shut. Picks up his guitar and goes out the front door of store U. C.*

> *Lady returns downstairs, laden with linen. The outer darkness moans through the door left open. She crosses to the door and a little outside it, peering both ways down the dark road. Then she comes in furiously, with an Italian curse, shutting the door with her foot or shoulder, and throws the linen down on counter. She crosses abruptly to cashbox, rings it open, and discovers theft. Slams drawer violently shut.*

Thief! Thief!

> *She turns to phone, lifts receiver. Holds it a moment, then slams it back into place. Wanders desolately back to the door, opens it and stands staring out into the starless night as the—*

SCENE DIMS OUT

> *as offstage guitar music is heard.*

Scene 2

Late that night. The bed linen is still on the counter.

Val enters the store, a little unsteadily, with his guitar, goes to the cashbox and rings it open. He counts some bills off a big wad and returns them to the cashbox and the larger wad to his pocket. Sudden footsteps above, light spills onto stair landing. He quickly moves away from the cashbox as Lady appears on the landing in a white sateen robe; she carries a flashlight.

LADY. Who's that?

> *Music fades out.*

VAL. —Me.

> *She turns the flashlight on his figure.*

LADY. Oh, my God, how you scared me!

VAL. You didn't expect me?

LADY. How'd I know it was you I heard come in?

VAL. I thought you give me a room here.

LADY. You left without letting me know if you took it or not.

> *She is descending the stairs into store, flashlight still on him.*

VAL. Catch me turning down something I get for nothing.

LADY. Well, you might have said something so I'd expect you or not.

VAL. I thought you took it for granted.

LADY. I don't take nothing for granted.

> *He starts back to the alcove.*

Wait!—I'm coming downstairs…

> *She descends with the flashlight beam on his face.*

VAL. You're blinding me with that flashlight.

> *She keeps the flashlight on him. He starts back again toward the alcove.*

LADY. The bed's not made because I didn't expect you.

VAL. That's all right.

LADY. I brought the linen downstairs and you'd cut out.

VAL. —Yeah, well—

> *She picks up linen on counter.*

Give me that stuff. I can make up my own rack. Tomorrow you'll have to get yourself a new clerk.

> *He takes it from her and goes again toward alcove.*

I had a lucky night. *(Exhibits a wad of bills.)*

LADY. *Hey!*

> *He stops near the curtain. She goes and turns on green shaded bulb over cashbox.*

—*Did you just open this cashbox!*

VAL. —Why you ask that?

LADY. I thought I heard it ring open a minute ago, that's why I come down here.

VAL. —In your—white satin—kimono?

LADY. *Did you just open the cashbox!!*

VAL. —I wonder who did if I didn't…

LADY. Nobody did if you didn't!

> *Lady opens cashbox and hurriedly counts money. She is trembling violently.*

VAL. How come you didn't lock the cash up in the safe this evening, Lady?

LADY. Sometimes I forget to.

VAL. That's careless.

LADY. —Why'd you open the cashbox when you come in?

VAL. I opened it twice this evening, once before I went out and again when I come back. I borrowed some money and put it back in the box an' got all this left over! *(Showing her the wad of bills.)* I beat a blackjack dealer five times straight. With this much loot I can retire for the season…

> *He returns money to pocket.*

LADY. *Chicken feed!*—I'm sorry for you.

VAL. You're sorry for me?

LADY. Yes. I'm sorry for you because nobody can help you. I was touched by your—strangeness, your strange talk.—That thing about birds with no feet so they have to sleep on the wind?—I said to myself, This boy is a bird with no feet so he has to sleep on the wind, and that softened my fool dago heart and I wanted to help you… Fool, me!—I got what I should of expected. You robbed me while I was upstairs to get sheets to make up your bed!

He starts out toward the door.

I guess I'm a fool to even feel disappointed.

VAL. *(Stops c.—drops linen on counter.)* You're disappointed in me. I was disappointed in you.

LADY. *(Coming from behind counter.)* —How did I disappoint you?

VAL. There wasn't no cot behind that curtain before. You put it back there for a purpose.

LADY. It was back there!—folded behind the mirror.

VAL. It wasn't back of no mirror when you told me three times to go and—

LADY. *(Cutting in.)* I left that money in the cashbox on purpose, to find out if I could trust you.

VAL. You got back th'—

LADY. No, no, no, I can't trust you, now I know I can't trust you, I got to trust anybody or I don't want him.

VAL. That's OK, I don't expect no character reference from you.

LADY. I'll give you a character reference. I'd say this boy's a peculiar talker! But I wouldn't say a real hard worker or honest. I'd say a peculiar slewfooter that sweettalks you while he's got his hand in the cashbox.

VAL. I took out less than you owed me.

LADY. Don't mix up the issue. I see through you, mister!

VAL. I see through you, Lady.

LADY. What d'you see through me?

VAL. You sure you want me to tell?

LADY. I'd love for you to.

VAL. —A not so young and not so satisfied woman, that hired a man off the highway to do double duty without paying overtime for it… I mean a store clerk days and a stud nights, and—

LADY. Oh, God, no…you cheap little—

Invectives fail her so she uses her fists, hammering at him with them. He seizes her wrists. …She struggles a few moments more, then collapses in chair R. of counter, sobbing. He lets go of her gently.

VAL. It's natural. You felt—lonely…

She sobs brokenly against the counter.

LADY. Why did you come back here?

VAL. To put back the money I took so you wouldn't remember me as not honest or grateful—

He picks up his guitar and starts to the U. C. door, nodding gravely. She catches her breath, rushes to intercept him, spreading her arms like a cross-bar over the door.

LADY. NO, NO, DON'T GO. …I NEED YOU!!!

He faces her for five beats. The true passion of her outcry touches him then, and he turns about and crosses to the alcove. …As he draws the curtain across it he looks back at her.

TO LIVE. …TO GO ON LIVING!!!

Offstage guitar music fades in. He closes the curtain and turns on the light behind it, making it translucent. Through an opening in the alcove entrance, we see him sitting down with his guitar. He begins to play softly. Lady picks up the linen and crosses to the alcove like a spellbound child. Just outside it she stops, frozen with uncertainty, a conflict of feelings. The stage darkens till only the curtain of the alcove is clearly visible as she enters the alcove.

CURTAIN

ACT III

SCENE 1

An early morning. The Saturday before Easter. The sleeping alcove is lighted.

Val smoking, half-dressed, on the edge of the cot. Lady comes running, panting downstairs, and calls out in a panicky, shrill whisper.

LADY. Val! Val, he's comin' downstairs!

VAL. *(Hoarse with sleep.)* Who's—what?

LADY. Jabe!

VAL. Jabe?

LADY. I swear he is, he's coming downstairs!

VAL. What of it?

LADY. Will you get up and put some clothes on? The damned nurse told him that he could come down in the store to check over the stock! You want him to catch you half-dressed on that bed there?

VAL. Don't he know I sleep here?

LADY. Nobody knows you sleep here but you and me.

Voices above.

NURSE. Don't hurry now!

LADY. Oh, God!—they've started.

Footsteps on stairs, slow, shuffling. The professional, nasal cheer of a nurse's voice.

NURSE. Take one step at a time.

LADY. *(Panicky.)* Get your shirt on! Come out!

NURSE. That's right. One step at a time, one step at a time, lean on my shoulder and take one step at a time.

Val rises, still dazed from sleep. Lady gasps and sweeps the curtain across the alcove just a moment before the decending figures enter the sightlines on the landing. Lady breathes like an exhausted runner, backing away from the alcove and assuming a forced smile. Jabe and the nurse, Miss Porter, appear on the landing of the stairs. They have a bizarre and awful appearance: the tall man, his rusty black suit hanging on him like an empty sack, his eyes burning malignantly from his yellow face, leaning on a stumpy little woman with bright-pink or orange hair, clad all in starched white, with a voice that purrs with the faintly contemptuous cheer and sweetness of those hired to care for the dying. The nurse continues:

Aw, now, just look at that, that nice bright sun comin' out.

LADY. Miss Porter? It's—it's cold down here!

JABE. What's she say?

NURSE. She says it's cold down there.

LADY. The—the—the air's not warm enough yet, the air's not heated!

NURSE. He's determined to come right down, Mrs. Torrance.

LADY. I know but—

NURSE. Wild horses couldn't hold him a minute longer.

JABE. *(Exhausted.)* —Let's—rest here a minute…

LADY. *(Eagerly.)* Yes! Rest there a minute!

NURSE. Okay.

> *Jabe sits down on a bench on landing under the artificial palm tree in the shaft of light. Jabe glares into the light like a fierce, dying old beast. There are sounds from the alcove. To cover them up, Lady keeps making startled, laughing sounds in her throat, half laughing, half panting, chafing her hands together at the foot of the stairs, and coughing falsely.*

JABE. Lady, what's wrong? Why are you so excited?

LADY. It seems like a miracle to me.

JABE. What seems like a miracle to you?

LADY. You coming downstairs.

JABE. You never thought I would come downstairs again?

LADY. Not this quick! Not as quick as this, Jabe! Did you think he would pick up as quick as this, Miss Porter?

Jabe rises.

NURSE. Ready?

JABE. Ready.

NURSE. He's doing fine, knock wood.

LADY. Yes, knock wood, knock wood!

> *She drums counter loudly with her knuckles. Val steps silently from behind the alcove curtain as the nurse and Jabe resume their slow, shuffling descent of the stairs. Lady moves back to* D. R. C.

You got to be careful not to over-do. You don't want another set-back. Ain't that right, Miss Porter?

NURSE. Well, it's my policy to mobilize the patient.

LADY. *(To Val in a shrill whisper.)* Coffee's boiling, take the coffee-pot off the burner!

> *She gives Val a panicky signal to go in the alcove.*

JABE. Who're you talking to, Lady?

LADY. To—to—to Val, the clerk! I told him to—get you a—chair!

JABE. Who's that?

LADY. Val, Val, the clerk, you know Val!

JABE. Not yet. I'm anxious to meet him. Where is he?

LADY. Right here, right here, here's Val!

> *Val returns from the alcove.*

JABE. He's here bright and early.

LADY. The early bird catches the worm!

JABE. That's right. Where is the worm?

NURSE. Careful! One step at a time, Mr. Torrance.

LADY. Saturday before Easter's our biggest salesday of the year, I mean second biggest, but sometimes it's even bigger than Christmas Eve! So I told Val to get here a half-hour early.

> *Jabe misses his step and stumbles to foot of stairs. Lady screams. Nurse rushes down to him. Val advances and raises the man to his feet.*

VAL. Here. Here.

71

LADY. Oh, my God.

NURSE. Oh, oh!

JABE. I'm all right.

NURSE. Are you sure?

JABE. Let me go!

>*He staggers to lean against counter, panting, glaring, with a malignant smile.*

LADY. Oh!

JABE. *(Crossing to L. C.)* This is the boy that works here?

LADY. Yes, this is the clerk I hired to help us out, Jabe.

JABE. How is he doing?

LADY. Fine, fine.

JABE. He's mighty good-looking. Do women give him much trouble?

LADY. When school lets out the high school girls are thick as flies in this store!

JABE. How about older women? Don't he attract older women? The older ones are the buyers, they got the money. They sweat it out of their husbands and throw it away! What's your salary, boy, how much do I pay you?

LADY. Twenty-two fifty a week.

JABE. You're getting him cheap.

VAL. I get—commissions.

JABE. Commissions?

VAL. Yes. One percent of all sales.

JABE. Oh? Oh? I didn't know about that.

LADY. I knew he would bring in trade and he brings it in.

JABE. I bet.

LADY. Val, get Jabe a chair, he ought to sit down.

JABE. No, I don't want to sit down. I want to take a look at the new confectionery.

>*He walks slowly toward confectionery R., assisted by nurse.*

LADY. Oh, yes, yes! Take a look at it! Val, Val, turn on the lights in

the confectionery! I want Jabe to see the way I done it over! I'm—
real—*proud*!

> *Val crosses to post* D. R. *and switches on light in confectionery.
> The bulbs in the arches and the juke-box light up.*

Go in and look at it, Jabe. I am real proud of it!

> *He stares at Lady a moment, then shuffles slowly into the
> spectral radiance of the confectionery. Lady moves* D. C. *At
> the same time a calliope becomes faintly audible and slowly
> but steadily builds. [Sound Cue 8, continuing.] Miss Porter
> goes with Jabe, holding his elbow.*

VAL. *(Returning to Lady.)* He looks like death.

LADY. *(Moves him away.)* Hush!

> *Val goes up above counter and stands in the shadows.*

NURSE. Well, isn't this artistic?

JABE. Yeh. Artistic as hell.

NURSE. I never seen anything like it before.

JABE. Nobody else did either.

NURSE. *(Coming back to* U. R. C.*)* Who done these decorations?

LADY. *(Defiantly.)* I did them, all by myself!

NURSE. What do you know. It sure is something artistic.

> *Calliope is now up loud.*

JABE. *(Coming back to* D. R.*)* Is there a circus or carnival in the
county?

LADY. What?

JABE. That sounds like a circus calliope on the highway.

LADY. That's no circus calliope. It's advertising the gala opening of
the Torrance Confectionery tonight!

JABE. Doing what did you say?

LADY. It's announcing the opening of our confectionery, it's going
all over Glorious Hill this morning and all over Sunset and Lyon
this afternoon. Hurry on down so you can see it go by the store.

> *She rushes excitedly to open the front door as the ragtime
> music of the calliope approaches.*

JABE. I married a live one, Miss Porter. How much does that damn thing cost me?

LADY. You'll be surprised how little. *(She is talking with an hysterical vivacity now.)* I hired it for a song!

JABE. How much of a song did you hire it for?

LADY. *(Closes door U. C.)* Next to nothing, seven-fifty an hour! And it covers three towns in Two River County!

> *Calliope fades out.*

JABE. *(With a muted ferocity.)* Miss Porter, I married a live one! Didn't I marry a live one?

> *He switches off lights in confectionery.*

Her daddy the Wop was just as much of a live one till he burned up.

> *Lady gasps as if struck.*

(With a slow, malignant grin.) He had a wine garden on the north shore of Moon Lake. The new confectionery sort of reminds me of it. But he made a mistake, he made a bad mistake, one time, selling liquor to niggers. We burned him out. We burned him out, house and orchard and vines and the Wop was burned up trying to fight the fire.

> *He turns.*

I think I better go up.

LADY. —did you say "WE"?

JABE. —I have a kind of a cramp…

NURSE. *(Taking his arm.)* Well, let's go up.

JABE. —Yes, I better go up…

> *They cross to stairs. Calliope fades in. [Sound Cue 8.]*

LADY. *(Almost shouting as she moves D. C.)* Jabe, did you say "WE" did it, did you say "WE" did it?

JABE. *(At foot of stairs—stops—turns.)* Yes, I said "We" did it. You heard me, Lady.

NURSE. One step at a time, one step at a time, take it easy.

> *They ascend gradually to the landing and above. The calliope passes directly before the store [Sound Cue 8] and a clown is*

heard shouting offstage.

CLOWN.   Don't forget tonight, folks, the gala opening of the Torrance Confectionery, free drinks and free favors, don't forget it, the gala opening of the confectionery.

> *Fade. Jabe and the Nurse disappear above the landing. Calliope gradually fades. A hoarse cry above. The nurse runs back downstairs, exclaiming—*

NURSE.   He's bleeding, he's having a hemm'rhage! *(Runs to phone.)* Dr. Buchanan's office! *(Turns again to Lady.)* Your husband is having a hemm'rhage!

> *Calliope is louder. Lady appears not to hear. She speaks to Val.*

LADY.   Did you hear what he said? He said "We" did it, "WE" burned—house—vines—orchard—"The Wop" burned fighting the fire…

THE SCENE DIMS OUT

Calliope fades out. [End of Sound Cue 8.]

SCENE 2

Sunset of the same day.

Val is alone. He is standing behind the counter with his guitar on counter in front of him. He crosses down to stage C. and stands with back to audience in the tense, frozen attitude of a wild animal listening to something that warns it of danger. After a moment he mutters something sharply, and his body relaxes, he takes out a cigarette and crosses to the store entrance, opens the door and stands looking out. It has been raining steadily and will rain again in a while, but right now it is clearing: the sun breaks through, suddenly, with great brilliance, and almost at the same instant, at some distance, a woman offstage cries out a great hoarse cry of terror and exaltation: the cry is repeated as she comes running nearer. Vee Talbott appears through the window as if blind and demented, with stiff, groping gestures, shielding her eyes with one arm as she feels along the store window for the entrance, gasping for breath. Val steps aside, taking hold of her arm to guide her into the store. For a few moments she leans weakly, blindly panting for breath against the oval glass of the U. C. door, then calls out—

VEE. I'm—*struck blind!*

VAL. You can't see?

VEE. —No! Nothing…

VAL. *(Assisting her to stool below counter.)* Set down here, Mrs. Talbott.

VEE. —Where?

VAL. *(Pushing her gently.)* Here.

    Vee sinks moaning onto stool.

What hurt your eyes, Mrs. Talbott, what happened to your eyes?

VEE. *(Drawing a long, deep breath.)* The vision I waited and prayed for all my life long!

VAL. You had a vision?

VEE. I saw the eyes of my Savior!—They struck me blind. *(Leans forward, clasping her eyes in anguish.)* Ohhhh, they burned out my eyes!

VAL. Lean back.

VEE. Eyeballs burn like fire...

VAL. *(Going off R.)* I'll get you something cold to put on your eyes.

VEE. I knew a vision was coming, oh, I had many signs!

VAL. *(In confectionery; gravely, gently.)* It must be a terrible shock to have a vision...

> *Vee, with the naiveté of a child as Val comes back to her carrying wet handkerchief. She sits on stool again.*

VEE. I *thought* I would see my Savior on the day of His passion, which was yesterday, Good Friday, that's when I expected to see Him. But I was mistaken, I was—disappointed. Yesterday passed and nothing, nothing much happened but—today—

> *Val places handkerchief over her eyes.*

this *afternoon,* somehow I pulled myself together and walked outdoors and started to go to pray in the empty church and meditate on the Rising of Christ tomorrow. Along the road as I walked, thinking about the mysteries of Easter, veils— *(Makes a long shuddering word out of "veils.")* seemed to drop off my eyes! Light, oh, light! I never have seen such brilliance! It *PRICKED* my eyeballs like *NEEDLES!*

VAL. —Light?

VEE. Yes, yes, light. YOU know, you know we live in light and shadow, that's, that's what we *live* in, a world of—*light* and—*shadow...*

VAL. Yes. In light and shadow.

> *He nods with complete understanding and agreement. They are like two children who have found life's meaning, simply and quietly, along a country road.*

VEE. A world of light and shadow is what we live in, and—it's—confusing...

> *A man is peering in at store window.*

VAL. Yeah, they—*do* get—*mixed...*

VEE. Well, and then— *(Hesitates to recapture her vision.)* I heard this

77

clap of thunder! Sky!—Split open!—And there in the split-open sky, I saw, I tell you, I *saw* the TWO HUGE BLAZING EYES OF JESUS CHRIST RISEN!—Not crucified but Risen! I mean Crucified and *then* RISEN!—The blazing eyes of Christ Risen! And then a great—

> *She raises both arms and makes a great sweeping motion to describe an apocalyptic disturbance of the atmosphere.*

—His hand!—*Invisible!*—I didn't *see* his hand! But it *touched* me—here!

> *She seizes Val's hand and presses it to her great heaving bosom.*

TALBOTT. *(Appearing R. in confectionery; furiously.)* VEE!

> *She starts up, throwing the compress from her eyes. Utters a sharp gasp and staggers backward, with terror and blasted ecstacy and dismay and belief all confused in her look.*

VEE. You!

TALBOTT. VEE!

VEE. *You!*

TALBOTT. *(Advancing.) VEE!*

VEE. *(Making two syllables of the word "eyes.")* —The Ey-es!

> *She collapses forward, falls to her knees, her arms thrown about Val. He seizes her to lift her. Two or three men are peering in at the store window.*

TALBOTT. *(Pushing Val away.)* Let go of her, don't put your hands on my wife!

> *He seizes her roughly and hauls her to the U. C. door. Val moves up to help Vee.*

Don't move. *(At door, to Val.)* I'm coming back.

VAL. I'm not goin' nowhere.

TALBOTT. *(As he goes off L. with Vee; to Dog.)* Dog, go in there with that boy.

VOICE. *(Outside.)* Sheriff caught him messin' with his wife.

> *Repeat: Another voice at a distance.*

> *Dog Hamma enters U. C. and stands silently beside the door while there is a continued murmur of excited voices on the street. The following scene should be under-played, played*

78

almost casually, like the performance of some familiar ritual.

VAL. What do you want?

Dog says nothing but removes from his pocket and opens a spring-blade knife and moves to D. R. Pee Wee enters through the open door U. C.

What do you—?

Pee Wee closes the door and silently stands beside it, opening a spring-blade knife. Val looks from one to the other.

—It's six o'clock. Store's closed.

The men chuckle like dry leaves rattling. Val crosses toward the U. C. door, is confronted by Talbott, stops short.

TALBOTT. Boy, I said stay here.

VAL. I'm not—goin' nowhere…

TALBOTT. Stand back under that light.

VAL. Which light?

TALBOTT. That light. *(Points.)*

Val goes behind counter.

I want to look at you while I run through some photos of men wanted.

VAL. I'm not wanted.

TALBOTT. A good-looking boy like you is always wanted.

Men chuckle. Val stands in hot light under green-shaded bulb. Talbott shuffles through photos removed from pocket.

—How tall are you, boy?

VAL. Never measured.

TALBOTT. How much do you weigh?

VAL. Never weighed.

TALBOTT. Got any scars or marks of identification on your face or body?

VAL. No, sir.

TALBOTT. Open your shirt.

VAL. What for?

He doesn't.

TALBOTT. Open his shirt for him, Pee Wee!

> *Pee Wee steps quickly forward and rips Val's shirt open to waist. Val starts forward. Men point knives. He draws back.*

That's right, stay there, boy. What did you do before?

> *Pee Wee sits on stairs.*

VAL. Before—what?

TALBOTT. Before you come here?

VAL. —Traveled and—played…

TALBOTT. Played?

DOG. *(Advancing to c.)* What?

PEE WEE. With wimmen?

> *Dog laughs.*

VAL. No. Played guitar—and sang…

> *Val touches guitar on counter.*

TALBOTT. Let me see that guitar.

VAL. Look at it. But don't touch it. I don't let nobody but musicians touch it.

> *Men come close.*

DOG. What're you smiling for, boy?

PEE WEE. He ain't smiling, his mouth's just twitching like a dead chicken's foot.

> *They laugh.*

TALBOTT. What is all that writing on the guitar?

VAL. —Names…

TALBOTT. What of?

VAL. Autographs of musicians dead and living.

> *Men read aloud the names printed on the guitar: Bessie Smith, Leadbelly, Woody Guthrie, Jelly Roll Morton, etc. They bend close to it, keeping the open knife blades pointed at Val's body; Dog touches neck of the guitar, draws it toward him. Val suddenly springs, with cat-like agility, onto the counter. He runs along it, kicking at their hands as they catch at his legs. The nurse runs down to the landing.*

NURSE. *What's going on?* I got a very sick man up there. *Hush!*

TALBOTT. *(At the same time, overlapping nurse.) Stop that!*

> *Nurse's voice fades out as she returns above.*

Dog! Pee Wee! You all stand back from that counter. Dog, why don't you an' Pee Wee go up an' see Jabe. Leave me straighten this boy out, go on, go on up.

PEE WEE. C'mon, Dawg…

> *They go upstairs. Val remains panting on counter. Sheriff Talbott sits in shoe-chair at R. window. In Talbott's manner is a curious, half-abashed gentleness when alone with the boy, as if he recognized the purity in him and was, truly, for the moment, ashamed of the sadism implicit in the occurrence.*

TALBOTT. Awright, boy. Git on down off th' counter, I ain't gonna touch y'r guitar.

> *Val jumps off counter still holding guitar.*

But I'm gonna tell you something. They's a certain county I know of which has a big sign at the county line that says, "Nigger, don't let the sun go down on you in this county." That's all it says, it don't threaten nothing, it just says, "Nigger, don't let the sun go down on you in this county!"

> *He chuckles hoarsely. Rises—a step toward Val.*

Well, son? You ain't a nigger and this is not that county, but, son, I want you to just imagine that you seen a sign that said to you: "Boy, don't let the sun rise on you in this county." I said "rise," not "go down" because it's too close to sunset for you to git packed an' move on before that. But I think if you value that instrument in your hands as much as you seem to, you'll simplify my job by not allowing the sun tomorrow to rise on you in this county. 'S that understood, now, boy?

> *Val stares at him, expressionless, panting.*

(Crossing to door.) I hope so. I don't like *violence.*

> *He looks back and nods at Val from the door. Then goes outside in the fiery afterglow of the sunset. Dogs bark in the distance. [Sound Cue 9.] Music fades in offstage—minor—guitar. Pause in which Val remains motionless, cradling guitar in his arms. Lights fade out.*

SCENE 3

Dogs and music fade out. Half an hour later. The lighting is less realistic than in the previous scenes of the play. The interior of the store is so dim that only the vertical lines of the pillars and such selected items as the palm tree on the stair-landing and the ghostly paper vineyard of the confectionery are plainly visible. The view through the great front window has virtually become the background of the action. A singing wind sweeps clouds before the moon so that the witch-like country brightens and dims and brightens again.

At rise, or when the stage is lighted again, it is empty but footsteps are descending the stairs as Dolly and Beulah rush into the store from U. C. and call out, in soft shouts—

DOLLY. Dawg?

BEULAH. Pee Wee?

EVA. *(Appearing on landing and calling down softly in the superior tone of a privileged attendant in a sick-chamber.)* Please don't *shout!*— Mr. Binnings and Mr. Hamma are upstairs sitting with Jabe...

> *She continues her descent. Then Sister appears, sobbing, on landing.*

—Come down carefully, Sister.

SISTER. Help me, I'm all to pieces...

> *Eva ignores this request and faces the two women.*

BEULAH. Has the bleedin' quit yit?

EVA. The hemorrhage seems to have stopped. Sister, Sister, pull yourself together, we all have to face these things sometime in life.

DOLLY. Has he sunk into a coma?

EVA. No. Cousin Jabe is conscious. Nurse Porter says his pulse is remarkably strong for a man that lost so much blood. Of course he's had a transfusion.

SISTER. Two of 'em.

EVA. *(Crossing to Dolly.)* Yais, an' they put him on glucose. His strength came back like magic.

82

BEULAH. She up there?

EVA. *Who?*

BEULAH. Lady!

EVA. *No!* When last reported she had just stepped into the Glorious Hill Beauty Parlor.

BEULAH. You don't mean it.

EVA. Ask Sister!

SISTER. She's planning to go ahead with—!

EVA. —The gala opening of the confectionery. Switch on the lights in there, Sister.

> *Sister crosses to post D. R. and switches on lights and moves off R. The decorated confectionery is lighted. Dolly and Beulah exclaim in awed voices.*

—Of course it's not normal behavior, it's downright lunacy, but still that's no excuse for it! And when she called up at five, about one hour ago, it wasn't to ask about Jabe, oh, no, she didn't mention his name. She asked if Ruby Lightfoot had delivered a case of Seagram's. Yais, she just shouted that question and hung up the phone.

> *She crosses and goes off R.*

BEULAH. *(Going into confectionery.) Oh, I understand, now! Now I see what she's up to!* Electric moon, cut-out silver paper stars and artificial vines? Why, it's her father's wine garden on Moon Lake she's turned this room into!

DOLLY. *(Suddenly as she sits in shoe-chair.) Here she comes, here she comes!*

> *Lady enters the store U. C. She wears a hooded rain cape and carries a large paper shopping bag and paper-carton box.*

LADY. Go on, ladies, don't stop, my ears are burning!

BEULAH. *(Coming in to U. R. C.)* —Lady, oh, Lady, Lady...

LADY. Why d'you speak my name in that pitiful voice, Beulah?

> *She throws back hood of cape, her eyes blazing and placing bag and box on counter.*

Val? Val! Where is that boy that works here?

> *Dolly shakes her head.*

I guess he's havin' a T-bone steak fo' ninety-five cents at the Blue Bird...

Sounds in confectionery.

Who's in the confectionery? Is that you, Val?

Temple sisters emerge and stalk past her.

Going, girls?

They go out of store U. C.

Yes, gone!

She laughs and throws off rain cape onto counter, revealing a low cut gown, triple strand of pearls, and a satin-ribboned corsage.

BEULAH. *(Sadly.)* ...How long have I known you, Lady?

LADY. *(Going behind counter—unpacks paper hats and whistles.)* A long time, Beulah. I think you remember when my people come here on a banana boat from Palermo, Sicily, by way of Caracas, Venezuela, yes, with a grind organ and a monkey my papa had bought in Venezuela. I was not much bigger than the monkey, ha ha! You remember the monkey? The man that sold Papa the monkey said it was a very young monkey, but he was a liar, it was a very old monkey, it was on its last legs, ha ha ha! But it was a well-dressed monkey. *(Coming around to R. of counter.)* It had a green velvet suit and a little red cap that it tipped and a tambourine that it passed around for money, ha ha ha. ...The grind organ played and the monkey danced in the sun, ha ha!—"O Sole Mio, da da da daaa...!" *(Sitting in chair at counter.)* —One day, the monkey danced too much in the sun and it was a very old monkey and it dropped dead. ...My papa, he turned to the people, he made them a bow and he said, "The show is over, the monkey is dead." Ha ha!

Slight pause. Then Dolly pipes up venomously—

DOLLY. Ain't it wonderful Lady can be so brave?

BEULAH. Yaiss, wonderful!

LADY. For me the show is not over, the monkey is not dead yet! *(Then suddenly—)* Val, is that you, Val?

Someone has entered the confectionery door, out of sight. Lady rushes forward but stops short as Carol appears R. She wears a trenchcoat.

DOLLY. Well, here's your first customer, Lady.

LADY. *(Going behind counter.)* —Carol, that room ain't open.

CAROL. There's a big sign outside that says "Open Tonite!"

LADY. It ain't open to you.

CAROL. I have to stay here a while. They stopped my car, you see, I don't have a license, my license has been revoked and I have to find someone to drive me across the river.

LADY. You can call a taxi.

CAROL. I heard that the boy works for you is leaving tonight and I—

LADY. *Who said he's leaving?*

CAROL. *(Crossing to counter.)* Sheriff Talbott. Suggested I get him to drive me over the river since he'd be crossing it too.

LADY. You got some mighty wrong information!

CAROL. Where is he? I don't see him?

LADY. Why d'you keep coming back here bothering that boy? He's not interested in you! Why would he be leaving here tonight?

> *Sound heard off* R. *as Lady comes from behind counter.*

Val, is that you, Val?

> *Conjure Man enters through confectionery, mumbling rapidly, holding out something. Beulah and Dolly take flight out the door with cries of revulsion.*

No conjure stuff, go away!

> *He starts to withdraw.*

CAROL. *(Crossing to* U. R. C.*)* Uncle! The Choctaw cry! I'll give you a dollar for it.

> *Lady turns away with a gasp, with a gesture of refusal. The Conjure Man nods, then throws back his turkey neck and utters a series of sharp barking sounds that rise to a sustained cry of great intensity and wildness. The cry produces a violent reaction in the building. Lady does not move but she catches her breath. Dog and Pee Wee run down the stairs with ad libs and hustle the Conjure Man out of the store, through confectionery, ignoring Lady. Val sweeps back the alcove curtain and*

appears as if the cry was his cue. He carries his guitar. Carol crosses downstage and speaks to the audience and to herself.

Something is still wild in the country! This country used to be wild, the men and women were wild and there was a wild sort of sweetness in their hearts, for each other, but now it's sick with neon, it's broken out sick, with neon, like most other places. ...I'll wait outside in my car. It's the fastest thing on wheels in Two River County!

She goes out of the store. Lady stares at Val with great asking eyes, a hand to her throat.

LADY. *(With false boldness.)* Well, ain't you going with her?

VAL. I'm going with no one I didn't come here with. And I come here with no one.

LADY. Then get into your white jacket. I need your services in that room there tonight.

Val regards her steadily for several beats.

(Clapping her hands together twice.) Move, move, stop goofing! The Delta Brilliant lets out in half 'n hour and they'll be driving up here. You got to shave ice for the set-ups!

VAL. *(As if he thought she'd gone crazy.)* "Shave ice for the set-ups"?

He moves up to counter.

LADY. Yes, an' call Ruby Lightfoot, tell her I need me a dozen more half-pints of Seagram's. They all call for Seven-and-Sevens. You know how t' sell bottle goods under a counter? It's OK. We're gonna git paid for protection. *(Gasps, touching her diaphragm.)* But one thing you gotta watch out for is servin' minors. Don't serve liquor to minors. Ask for his driver's license if they's any doubt. Anybody born earlier than— let's see—Oh, I'll figure it later. Hey! Move! Move! Stop goofing!

Val puts guitar on counter, as he reaches out to catch hold of her bare arm and he pulls her to him and grips her arms.

Hey!

VAL. Will you quit thrashin' around like a catfish?

LADY. Go git in y'r white jacket an'—

VAL. Sit down. I want to talk to you.

LADY. I don't have time.

VAL. I got to reason with you.

LADY. It's not possible to.

VAL. You can't open a night-place here this night.

LADY. You bet your sweet life I'm *going* to!

VAL. Not *me*, not *my* sweet life!

LADY. I'm betting *my* life on it! Sweet or *not* sweet, I'm—

VAL. Yours is yours, mine is mine…

    He releases her with a sad shrug.

LADY. You don't get the point, huh? There's a man up there that set fire to my father's wine garden and I lost my life in it, yeah, I lost my life in it, *three* lives was lost in it, two *born* lives and *one—not*. …I was made to commit a *murder* by him up there! *(Has frozen momentarily.)* —I want that man to see the wine garden come open again when he's dying! I want him to hear it coming open again here tonight! While he's dying. It's necessary, no power on earth can stop it. Hell, I don't even want it, it's just necessary, it's just something's got to be done to square things away, to, to, to—be *not defeated*! *You get me? Just to be not defeated!* Ah, oh, I won't be defeated, not again, in my life! *(Embraces him.)* Thank you for staying here with me!—God bless you for it. …Now please go and get in your white jacket…

    The tension is momentarily relieved by a breathless sob. She makes an odd, awkward gesture, almost crouching in a bow to him, but her eyes blind… Val looks at her as if he were trying to decide between a natural sensibility of heart and what his life's taught him since he left Witches Bayou. Then he sighs again, with the same slight, sad shrug, and crosses into alcove to put on a jacket and remove from under his cot a cheap suitcase with his belongings. Lady takes paper hats and whistles from counter, crosses into confectionery and puts them on the tables, then starts back, but stops short as she sees Val come out of alcove with his snakeskin jacket and suitcase.

That's not your white jacket, that's that snakeskin jacket you had on when you come here.

VAL. I come and I go in this jacket.

LADY. *Go*, did you say?

87

VAL. Yes, ma'am, I did, I said go. All that stays to be settled is a little matter of wages.

> *The dreaded thing's happened to her. This is what they call "the moment of truth" in the bull ring, when the matador goes in over the horns of the bull to plant the mortal sword-thrust.*

LADY. —So you're—cutting out, are you?

VAL. My gear's all packed. I'm catchin' the Southbound bus.

LADY. Uh-huh, in a pig's eye. You're not conning me, mister. She's waiting for you outside in her high-powered car and you're—

> *Nurse Porter calls from off, upstairs.*

NURSE. Mrs. Torrance, are you down there?

LADY. *(Crossing to foot of stairs.)* Yeah. I'm here. I'm back.

> *Val crosses to c., putting suitcase down in front of counter.*

NURSE. Can I talk to you up here about Mr. Torrance?

LADY. *(Shouting to nurse.)* I'll be up in a minute.

> *Lady turns to Val.*

OK, now, mister. You're scared about something, ain't you.

VAL. I been threatened with violence if I stay here.

LADY. I got paid-for protection in this county, plenty paid for it, and it covers you too.

VAL. No, ma'am. My time is up here.

LADY. Y'say that like you'd served a sentence in jail.

VAL. I got in deeper than I meant to, Lady.

LADY. Yeah, and how about me?

VAL. *(Going to her.)* I would of cut out before you got back to the store, but I wanted to tell you something I never told no one before.

> *He places hand on her shoulder.*

I feel a true love for you, Lady!

> *He kisses her.*

I'll wait for you out of this county, just name the time and the...

LADY. *(Moves back.)* Oh, don't talk about love, not to me, because I know what you are. It's easy to say "Love, Love!" with fast and free transportation waiting right out the door for you!

VAL. D'you remember some things I told you about me the night we met here?

LADY. *(Crossing to R. C.)* Yeah, I remember. Yeah, temperature of a dog. And some bird without legs so it had to sleep on the wind!

VAL. *(Through her speech.)* Naw, not that; not that.

LADY. And how you could burn down a woman? I said "Bull!" I take that back. You can! You can burn down a woman and stamp on her ashes to make sure that fire is put out!

VAL. I mean what I said about gettin' away from...

LADY. How long've you held this first steady job in your life?

VAL. How long? too long!

LADY. Four months and five days, mister. How much pay have you took?

VAL. I told you to keep out all but—

LADY. All but y'r living expenses. Y'know how much you got coming? IF you get it? You got five hundred and eighty-six bucks coming to you, not chicken feed, that. But, mister— *(Gasps for breath.)* if you try to walk out on me, now, tonight, without notice!—You're going to get just nothing! A great big zero...

> *Somebody knocks and hollers off R.: "Hey! You open?" She rushes toward it shouting,*

CLOSED! CLOSED! GO AWAY!

> *Val crosses to the cashbox. She turns back toward him, gasps.*

Now you watch your next move and I'll watch mine. You open that cashbox and I swear I'll throw open that door and holler, "Clerk's robbing the store!"

VAL. —Lady?

LADY. *(Fiercely.)* Hanh?

VAL. —Nothing, you've—blown your stack. I will go without pay.

LADY. *(Coming to C.)* Then you ain't understood me! With or without pay, you're staying!

VAL. I've got my gear.

> *He picks up suitcase. She rushes to seize his guitar.*

LADY. Then I'll go up and git mine! And take this with me, just t' make sure you wait till I'm—

She moves back to R. C. He puts suitcase down.

VAL. *(Advancing toward her.)* Lady, what're you—?

LADY. *(Entreating with guitar raised.)* Don't—!

VAL. —Doing with—

LADY. —*Don't!*

VAL. —my guitar!

LADY. *Holding it for security while I—*

VAL. Lady, you been a lunatic since this morning!

LADY. Longer, longer than morning! I'm going to keep hold of your "life companion" while I pack! I am! I am goin' to pack an' go, if you go, where you go!

He makes a move toward her. She crosses below and around to counter.

You didn't think so, you actually didn't think so? What was I going to do, in your opinion? What, in your opinion, would I be doing? Stay on here in a store full of bottles and boxes while you go far, while you go fast and far, without me having your—forwarding address!—even?

VAL. I'll—give you a forwarding address…

LADY. Thanks, oh, thanks! Would I take your forwarding address back of that curtain? "Oh, dear forwarding address, hold me, kiss me, be faithful!"

Jabe knocks above. She utters grotesque, stifled cry. Presses fist to mouth. He advances cautiously, hand stretched toward the guitar. She retreats above to U. R. C., biting lip, eyes flaring.

Stay back! You want me to smash it!

VAL. *(D. C.)* He's—knocking for you…

LADY. I know! Death's knocking for me! Don't you think I hear him, knock, knock, knock? It sounds like what it is! Bones knocking bones… Ask me how it felt to be coupled with death up there, and I can tell you. My skin crawled when he touched me. But I endured it. I guess my heart knew that somebody must be coming to take me out of this hell! You did. You came. Now look at me! I'm alive once more!

> *Convulsive sobbing controlled, she continues more calmly and harshly.*

—*I won't wither in dark!* Got that through your skull? Now. Listen! Everything in this rotten store is yours, not just your pay, but everything Death's scraped together down here!—but Death has got to die before we can go…—You got that memorized, now?—Then get into your white jacket!—*Tonight is the gala opening—* *(Rushes through confectionery.) of the confectionery—*

> *Val runs and seizes her arm holding guitar. She breaks violently free.*

Smash me against a rock and I'll smash your guitar! I will, if you—

> *Nurse calls from upstairs.*

NURSE. Mrs. Torrance! Mrs. Torrance!

LADY. *Oh, Miss Porter!*

> *She motions Val back. He retreats into alcove. Lady puts guitar down beside jukebox. Nurse is descending the stairs. She carries a purse.*

NURSE. *(Descending watchfully.)* You been out a long time.

LADY. *(Moving U. R. C.)* Yeah, well, I had lots of—

> *Her voice expires breathlessly. She stares fiercely, blindly, into the other's hard face.*

NURSE. —of what?

LADY. Things to—things to—take care of… *(Draws a deep, shuddering breath, clenched fist to her bosom.)*

NURSE. Didn't I hear you shouting to someone just now?

LADY. —Uh-huh. Some drunk tourist made a fuss because I wouldn't sell him no—liquor…

NURSE. *(Crossing to the door.)* Oh. Mr. Torrance is sleeping under medication.

LADY. That's good.

> *She sits in shoe-fitting chair U. R.*

NURSE. I gave him a hypo at five.

LADY. —Don't all that morphine weaken the heart, Miss Porter?

NURSE. Gradually, yes.

LADY. How long does it usually take for them to let go?

NURSE. It varies according to the age of the patient and the condition his heart's in. Why?

LADY. Miss Porter, don't people sort of help them let go?

NURSE. How do you mean, Mrs. Torrance?

LADY. Shorten their suffering for them?

NURSE. Oh, I see what you mean. *(Snaps her purse shut.)* —I see what you mean, Mrs. Torrance. But killing is killing regardless of circumstances.

LADY. Nobody said killing.

NURSE. You said "shorten their suffering."

LADY. Yes, like merciful people shorten an animal's suffering when he's…

NURSE. A human being is not the same as an animal, Mrs. Torrance. And I don't hold with what they call—

LADY. *(Overlapping.) Don't give me a sermon*, Miss Porter. I just wanted to know if—

NURSE. *(Overlapping.)* I'm not giving a sermon. I just answered your question. If you want to get somebody to shorten your husband's life—

LADY. *(Jumps up, overlapping.)* Why, how dare you say that I—

NURSE. I'll be back at ten-thirty.

LADY. Don't!

NURSE. What?

LADY. *(Crossing behind counter.)* Don't come back at ten-thirty, don't come back.

NURSE. I'm always discharged by the doctors on my cases.

LADY. This time you're being discharged by the patient's wife.

NURSE. That's something we'll have to discuss with Dr. Buchanan.

LADY. I'll call him myself about it. I don't like you. I don't think you belong in the nursing profession, you have cold eyes, I think you like to watch pain!

NURSE. I know why you don't like my eyes. You don't like my eyes because you know they see clear.

LADY. Why are you staring at *me*?

NURSE. I'm not staring at you, I'm staring at that curtain. There's something burning in there, smoke's coming out!

> *Nurse starts toward alcove.*

LADY. Oh, no, you don't.

> *Lady seizes her arm. Nurse pushes her roughly aside and crosses to the curtain. Val rises from cot, opens the curtain and faces her coolly.*

NURSE. Oh!

> *She turns to Lady.*

—the moment I looked at you when I was called on this case last Friday morning I knew that you were pregnant.

> *Lady gasps.*

I also knew the moment I looked at your husband it wasn't by him.

> *She stalks to the door u. c. Lady suddenly cries out—*

LADY. Thank you for telling me what I hoped for is true.

NURSE. You don't seem to have any shame.

LADY. *(Exalted.)* No. I don't have shame. I have—*great*—*joy!*

NURSE. *(Venomously.)* Then why don't you get the calliope and the clown to make the announcement?

LADY. You do it for me, save me the money! Make the announcement, all over!

> *Nurse goes out u. c., leaving door open. Val crosses swiftly to the door and closes it. Then he advances toward her, saying—*

VAL. Is it true what she said?

> *Lady moves as if stunned to the counter. The stunned look gradually turns to a look of wonder. On the counter is a heap of silver and gold paper hats and trumpets for the gala opening of the confectionery.*

(In a hoarse whisper.) Is it true or not true, what that woman told you?

LADY. You sound like a scared little boy.

VAL. She's gone out to tell.

Pause.

LADY. You gotta go now—it's dangerous for you to stay here. ...Take your pay out of the cashbox, you can go. Take the keys to my car, cross the river into some other county. You've done what you came here to do...

VAL. —It's true then, it's—?

LADY. *(Sitting in chair by counter.)* True as God's word! I have life in my body, this dead tree, my body, has burst in flower! You've given me life, you can go!

> *He crouches down gravely opposite her, gently takes hold of her knotted fingers and draws them to his lips, breathing on them as if to warm them. She sits bolt upright, tense, blind as a clairvoyant.*

VAL. —Why didn't you tell me before?

LADY. —When a woman's been childless as long as I've been childless, it's hard to believe that you're still able to bear!—We used to have a little fig tree between the house and the orchard. It never bore any fruit, they said it was barren. Time went by it, spring after useless spring, and it almost started to—die... Then one day I discovered a small green fig on the tree they said wouldn't bear!

> *She is clasping a gilt paper horn.*

I ran through the orchard. I ran through the wine garden shouting, "Oh, Father, it's going to bear, the fig tree is going to bear!"—It seemed such a wonderful thing, after those ten barren springs, for the little fig tree to bear, it called for a celebration—I ran to a closet, I opened a box that we kept Christmas ornaments in!—I took them out, glass bells, glass birds, tinsel, icicles, stars... And I hung the little tree with them, I decorated the fig tree with glass bells and glass birds, and silver icicles and stars, because it won the battle and it would bear! *(Rises, ecstatic.)* Unpack the box! Unpack the box with the Christmas ornaments in it, put them on me, glass bells and glass birds and stars and tinsel and snow!

> *In a sort of delirium she runs upstairs to the landing, crying out.*

Because I've won, I've won, Mr. Death, I'm going to bear!

VAL. *(Shouts softly.)* Lady—Lady!

> *Then suddenly she falters, catches her breath in a shocked gasp and awkwardly retreats to the stairs. Then she turns, screaming, and runs back down them, her cries dying out as she arrives at the floor level, she retreats haltingly as a blind person, a hand stretched out to Val, as slow, clumping footsteps and hoarse breathing are heard on the stairs. She moans—*

LADY. —Oh, God. …What did I do?…

> *Jabe appears on the landing, by the artificial palm tree in its dully lustrous green jardiniere. A stained purple robe hangs loosely about his wasted, yellowed frame. He is death's self, and malignancy, as he peers, crouching, down into the store's dimness to discover his quarry.*

JABE. Buzzards! Buzzards!

> *Clutching the railing of the landing, he raises the other hand holding a revolver and fires down into the store. Lady screams and rushes to cover Val's motionless figure with hers. Jabe scrambles down a few steps and fires again and the bullet strikes her, expelling her breath in a great "Hah!" She turns to face him, still covering Val with her body, her face with all the passions and secrets of life and death in it now, her fierce eyes blazing, knowing, and still defying. But the revolver is empty, and Jabe hurls it toward them, descends and passes them, shouting out hoarsely.*

I'll have him killed! I burned your father and I'll have him killed!

> *He opens the door U. C. and rushes out onto the road shouting hoarsely.*

The clerk is robbing the store, he shot my wife, the clerk is robbing the store, he killed my wife!

VAL. —Did it—?

> *Clamor builds outside.*

LADY. *Lock the door!*

> *He rushes to bolt the front door; at the same time she grasps hold of arch post R. C.*

VAL. Did it?

He returns with the terror of a hunted animal, panting with it.

LADY. *Go! Quick! The side way!* Go! Go! *(Points off* R.*)*

VAL. Did it?!

LADY. *(Inclines her head slightly and says—)* The show is over, the monkey is dead...

> *Then she moves into the confectionery and falls. Val bends over her for a moment—then Dog enters from* R. *Val turns— hesitates a second then dashes to front door, where other men have arrived forcing the door open. Men are in the store, and the dark is full of hoarse, shouting voices. They grab Val and drag him off* R. *Immediately after they run off, there is an explosion of voices about the store, offstage. The motors start and fade out as they go. The baying of chain-gang dogs in pursuit is heard. [Sound Cue 10.] As they capture Val and take him off* R., *two of the men remain in the store.*

1ST MAN. *Hey, git some rope!*

2ND MAN. Don't need no rope for that boy, they're gonna tear off his clothes an' throw th' son-of-a-bitch to the chain-gang dogs!

> *He has already crossed behind the counter.*

You watch out that window, bud, while I empty this God damned cashbox.

1ST MAN. *Somebody's out there!*

2ND MAN. *(As he rushes out through the confectionery.)* C'mon, we'll split it outside!

> *1st man follows him off* R. *Carol enters* U. C. *as dog-baying rises in ferocity. She cries:*

CAROL. RUN!—RUN!—RUN!

> *She says this in a feeling of not believing it would help the runner. She crosses to stool below counter and sits, then crouches over in vicarious agony as the sound of pursuit reaches a climax... Dog baying fades out as the Conjure Man enters* D. R. *carrying the snakeskin jacket and crosses to Carol, who looks up as he holds the jacket up with his rapid, toothless mumble of excitement.*

What have you got there, Uncle? OH! His snakeskin jacket!—I'll give you a gold ring for it. It ought to be passed on to me.

> *Offstage guitar music fades in. The exchange is made, a simple ceremony. The Negro sits in the chair at counter and examines the ring. Shivering, she puts the jacket on, saying—as she moves* D. C.—

Wild things leave skins behind them, they leave clean skins and teeth and white bones behind them, and these are tokens passed from one to another, so that the fugitive kind can always follow their kind…

> *She draws the jacket about her as if she were cold, nods to the old Negro. Then she crosses off* R., *pausing halfway as Sheriff Talbott enters* R.

TALBOTT. Don't no one move, don't move!

> *Music stops short. She crosses directly past him as if she no longer saw him, and out, off* R. *He shouts furiously—*

Stay here!

> *Her laughter rings outside. He follows the girl shouting—*

Stop! Stop!

> *Silence. The Conjure Man looks up with a secret smile as…*

THE CURTAIN FALLS SLOWLY

PROPERTY LIST

(Use this space to make props lists for your production)

SOUND CUES

Band	Cue	Page	Effect
1	1	8	Train whistle in the distance
2	2	20	Sound of car coming to stop
3	3	27	Dog bays in the distance
4	4	28	Sound of car going off fast
5	5	39	Mule team laboring to pull big truck back on pavement
6	6	43	Sound of car horn is heard repeatedly 6 or 7 times
7	7	59	Sound of baying dogs, to crescendo of single savage note, then 2 shots are fired, baying fades
8	8	73-75	Sound of calliope
9	9	81	Sound of dogs barking in the distance
10	10	96	Cars start and fade off, sound of baying dogs

Note on Songs/Recordings, Images, or Other Production Design Elements

Be advised that Dramatists Play Service, Inc., neither holds the rights to nor grants permission to use any songs, recordings, images, or other design elements mentioned in the play. It is the responsibility of the producing theater/organization to obtain permission of the copyright owner(s) for any such use. Additional royalty fees may apply for the right to use copyrighted materials.

For any songs/recordings, images, or other design elements mentioned in the play, works in the public domain may be substituted. It is the producing theater/organization's responsibility to ensure the substituted work is indeed in the public domain. Dramatists Play Service, Inc., cannot advise as to whether or not a song/arrangement/recording, image, or other design element is in the public domain.